The Usborne

Nature Sticker Book

Trees, Birds & Flowers

How to use this book

There are over 300 illustrations of trees, birds and flowers in this book. Using the descriptions and the pictures, try to match each sticker to the right entry. If you need help, a checklist at the end of each section tells you which sticker goes where. You can also use this book as a spotter's handbook to make a note of the birds, trees and flowers you have seen.

At the beginning of each section you will find a diagram naming the main parts of a tree, bird or flower, and there are explanations of other useful words at the end of the tree and flower sections, too. Some of the bird and flower descriptions also include helpful pronunciation guides, for example Capercaillie ("kappa-kale-ee").

Photographs: Cover (front):

Lime leaves © Westend61 / Alamy; Mistle thrushes © Kim Taylor / Warren Photographic; Wildflower meadow © Organics image library / Alamy; Welsh poppy © GardenWorld Images / Alamy; Back cover: Blue tit © Alan Williams / Alamy

The material in this booker was originally published separately as the "Trees Sticker Book", "Birds Sticker Book" and "Flowers Sticker Book".

This edition first published in 2007 by Usborne Publishing Ltd, Usborne House, 83–85 Saffron Hill, London EC1N 8RT, England. www.usborne.com

The Usborne Nature Sticker Book

Trees, Birds & Flowers

Jane Chisholm, Phillip Clarke and Lisa Miles

Designed by:
Leonard Le Rolland and Karen Tomlins

Edited by Phillip Clarke

Illustrated by:
Aziz Khan, Annabel Milne, Peter Stebbing,
Trevor Boyer, Sue Testar, Joyce Bee,
Hilary Burn, William Giles,
Christine Howes and Ian Jackson

Consultants:
Derek Patch, Tree Advice Trust
Peter Holden, RSPB
Dr Mark A. Spencer, Natural History Museum

Pines

Pine trees are evergreen conifers. This means they don't lose all their leaves at once in winter, and their fruits are woody cones. They have thin, needle-like leaves, in pairs or in groups of three or five.

Shore pine

Height: 23m (75ft)

Shore pines are tall, narrow, fast-growing trees with small cones in clusters. They have yellow-green needles in pairs on twisted shoots, scaly bark, and sticky, bullet-shaped buds.

WHEN ....

WHERE ....

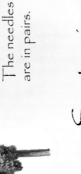

The needles are in pairs.

Shore pine

The long, bare trunk of a Scots pine is red near the top.

Scots pine

Height: 35m (115ft)

This tree isn't found only in Scotland, but all across Europe. It has short, blue-green paired needles and small, pointed buds. The bark is red at the top, grey and furrowed below. Young trees are pointed in shape, becoming flat-topped later.

WHEN ....

WHERE ....

Young shoot, seen early in summer.

The green, pointed cones turn brown in the second year.

Corsican pine

Height: 36m (118ft)

Tall, fast-growing trees, Corsican pines have branches at regular intervals. They have long, dark-green, paired needles, onion-shaped buds and large, lop-sided brown cones. Their bark is blackish.

WHEN ....

WHERE ....

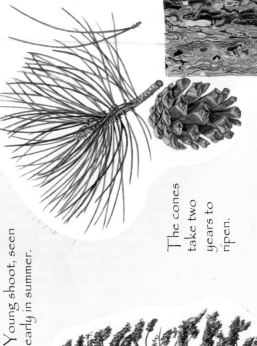

The cones take two years to ripen.

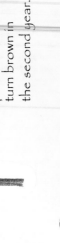

Corsican pine

Maritime pine

Height: 22m (72ft)

Native to the Mediterranean, this tree is often found in sandy soils near the sea. It has long, stout, grey-green paired needles, torpedo-shaped buds, and long, shiny brown cones grouped in clusters. Its long, bare trunk has rugged bark.

WHEN ....

WHERE ....

Monterey pine

The cones are uneven at the base.

Swiss stone pine

Height: 17m (56ft)

Smaller than many other pines, and shaped rather like a cone, Swiss stone pines are found in the Alps and other mountainous regions. They have dense, stiff needles in fives, and small, pointed, sticky buds. Their cones are shaped rather like eggs, and contain seeds that ripen and fall in their third year.

WHEN ....

WHERE ....

Needles in a group of five

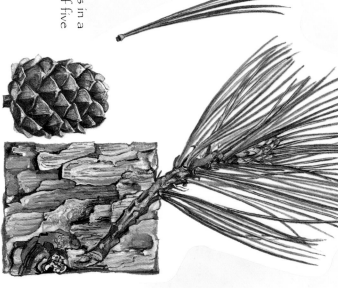

Swiss stone pine

Monterey pine

Height: 30m (98ft)

Originally from California, this is a broad-crowned tree with many branches. It has slender, grass-green needles in threes and large, pointed, sticky buds. Its squat cones grow flat against the branches, staying on the tree for many years.

WHEN ....

WHERE ....

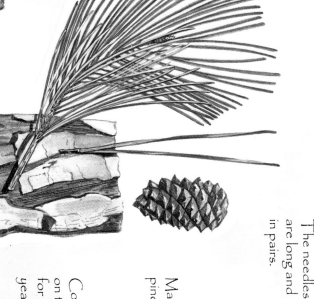

Maritime pine

The needles are long and in pairs.

Cones stay on the tree for several years.

7

Spruces, firs and hemlocks

Spruces, firs and hemlocks are all evergreen conifers, bearing cones and individual needles. The yew is similar, but with red berries instead of cones.

The cones have papery scales with crinkled edges.

Grey, scaly bark which flakes off in "plates".

Sitka spruce

Height: 35m (115ft)

Sitka spruces are narrow, cone-shaped trees with very prickly blue-green needles and plump yellow buds. When the needles are pulled off, they leave small knobs on yellow twigs.

WHEN ....
WHERE ....

Sitka spruce

Norway spruce

Height: 30m (98ft)

Traditionally used as Christmas trees, Norway spruces have a regular, conical shape, with prickly, dark-green needles, and cones which hang down. When the needles are pulled off, they leave peg-like bumps on brown twigs.

WHEN ....
WHERE ....

The scales of the cones are tightly closed.

Norway spruce

European silver fir

The cones are tall and upright.

European silver fir

The cones have leaf-like structures, called bracts, at the bases of the scales.

European silver fir

Height: 40m (131ft)

Rare in Britain, but common in central Europe, this is a tall, narrow tree, with flat needles, green above and silvery below. Its needles drop, leaving flat, round scars on the twigs. The cones shed their scales when ripe.

WHEN ....
WHERE ....

Noble fir

Height: 37m (121ft)

Noble firs have level branches and dense, silver-blue needles, curving upwards. They have enormous shaggy cones with down-turned bracts. The scales of the cones fall off, leaving tall spikes.

WHEN ....

WHERE ....

Noble fir cones grow up to 20cm (8in) long.

Yew

Height: 15m (50ft)

You may see a yew tree in a churchyard, or as part of a hedge. It has a short, stout trunk; wide, spreading branches; orange-brown, flaking bark and red, berry-like fruits. Its broad needles are dark green above and yellowish-green below.

WHEN ....

WHERE ....

Yew leaves and seeds are poisonous.

Douglas fir

Height: 40m (131ft)

This tree has soft needles, long, pointed copper-brown buds, and light-brown hanging cones with three-pointed bracts. When the tree is old, its bark becomes thick and corky.

WHEN ....

WHERE ....

Douglas fir cones have three-pointed bracts.

Western hemlock

Height: 35m (115ft)

This tree is originally from the western part of North America. It has smooth, brown, scaly bark, drooping branch tips and top shoots with small cones. Its needles vary in length, and are green above and silver below.

WHEN ....

WHERE ....

The cones have a few rounded scales.

Cedars and larches

Cedars and larches are conifers, but not all are evergreen. Most of the trees shown here have single needles on the end of their shoots and in bunches on the older shoots.

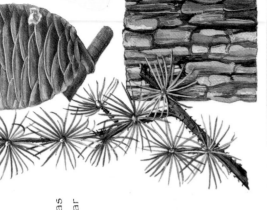

Cone with sunken top

Atlas cedar

Height: 25m (82ft)

Atlas cedars are large, spreading trees, originally from the Atlas mountains of Morocco. Often seen in parks and gardens, their branches rise upwards, and they have large, upright, barrel-shaped cones with sunken tops.

WHEN ....

WHERE ....

Atlas cedar

The leaves are blue-green in the common garden variety, dark-green in the wild.

Cedar of Lebanon

Height: 30m (98ft)

Cedars of Lebanon are similar to Atlas cedars, except that their cones don't have sunken tops. They have level branches, with masses of dense foliage, giving the impression of flat "tables" of leaves.

WHEN ....

WHERE ....

Cedar of Lebanon

Cone covered with sticky resin

New shoots with single needles

Older shoot with needles in bunches

Deodar cedar

Deodar cedar

Height: 23m (76ft)

Deodar cedars have soft, pale-green leaves, a pointed crown, and large, barrel-shaped cones with slightly sunken tops. The top shoots and branches droop.

WHEN ....

WHERE ....

European larch

Height: 38m (125ft)

European larches have bunches of soft, light-green needles. They are deciduous, which means the needles fall in winter. After they turn yellow and fall, they leave small knobs on the twigs. The trees have small, flexible, egg-shaped cones and reddish female flowers. (In some types of tree, such as the larch or the ash, male and female flowers grow on separate trees.)

WHEN ....

WHERE ....

Japanese larch

Japanese larches have stout branches.

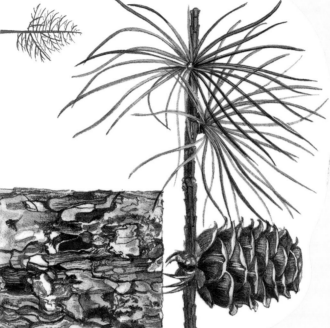

The edges of the scales of the cones turn backwards.

European larches have fine, light branches.

Japanese larch

Height: 35m (115ft)

This Japanese tree is also grown in Europe. It is deciduous, with bunches of blue-green needles, which fall in winter, leaving orange twigs. Its female flowers are pinkish-green and it has small, flower-like cones.

WHEN ....

WHERE ....

Japanese red cedar

Height: 30m (98ft)

Japanese red cedars are tall, narrow, cone-shaped and evergreen with reddish-brown, peeling bark. They have long, bright-green, spiky scale-like needles which curve away from the twig. Their cones are green and spiky, turning brown when ripe.

WHEN ....

WHERE ....

Ripe cone

Reddish-brown peeling bark

Japanese red cedar

Redwoods and cypresses

The trees on these two pages are all conifers. They are all evergreen, with sprays of scale-like leaves, apart from the dawn redwood and swamp cypress.

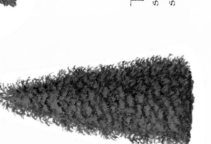

Cone

Western red cedar

Height: 30m (98ft)

Western red cedars are actually cypress trees, originally found in northwestern parts of North America. They have small, flower-shaped cones, and smooth, finely furrowed bark. Their twigs are covered with flattened sprays of scented, scale-like leaves.

The leaves are dark, shiny green above and streaked white below.

Western red cedar

WHEN ....

WHERE ....

Monterey cypress

Monterey cypress

Height: 25m (82ft)

Originally from California, Monterey cypresses have dense sprays of small, scale-like leaves and large, purplish-brown, rounded cones with knobs on their scales. The young trees are column-shaped, becoming flat-topped when old, and their bark is often peeling.

WHEN ....

WHERE ....

The leaves, when crushed, smell of lemon.

The cone looks like a berry.

Juniper

Juniper

Height: 20m (65ft)

Junipers can be trees or bushes. They have prickly, blue-green needles which smell strongly when crushed. The needles come in threes, with a white band on their upper surfaces. Juniper cones look like berries and turn purplish-black in their second year.

WHEN ....

WHERE ....

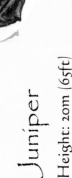

Giant sequoia

Height: 30–90m (100–300ft)

Also called sierra redwood, wellingtonia or just "bigtree", these can grow to be the world's most massive trees. They have soft, thick, deeply furrowed bark, upswept branches, and long-stalked, round, corky cones. The cones have diamond-shaped scales which wrinkle when they ripen.

WHEN ....

WHERE ....

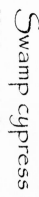

Dawn redwood

The cones grow on long stalks.

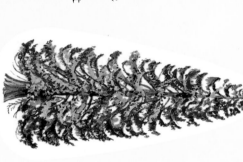

Giant sequoia

Giant sequoia leaves are deep green, scale-like and pointed.

Dawn redwood

Height: 20m (66ft)

Dawn redwoods are deciduous conifers, with soft, light-green needles which turn reddish in autumn. You'll rarely see cones, but when they appear, they are small bobbles on long stalks. The bark is orange when the tree is young, and flaking and furrowed in older trees.

WHEN ....

WHERE ....

Swamp cypress

Height: 20m (66ft)

This tree is so called because it can grow in swampy places. It has a triangular crown and soft, feathery, light-green needles that drop in winter, leaving orange twigs. Its cones are round and purplish-brown. Its bark is reddish-brown, often peeling, and forms a spiral pattern.

WHEN ....

WHERE ....

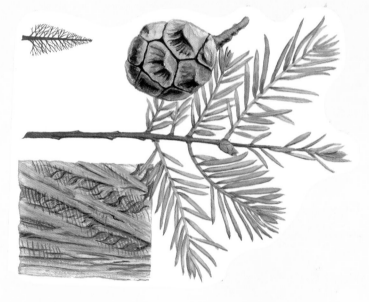

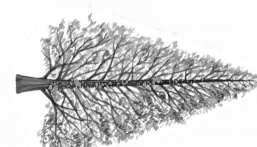

Swamp cypress

The leaves appear very late and the foliage is not dense.

13

Simple leaves

All these trees are broadleaved: they have wide, flat, simple leaves (simple leaves are not divided into sections, or "leaflets").

Southern beech

Height: 20m (66ft)

Southern beeches originated in the southern hemisphere, but have been planted in Europe. They have narrow, oval leaves, with finely-toothed edges and many obvious veins. The fruit is deep-green and prickly. The bark is silver-grey.

WHEN ....

WHERE ....

The southern beech has a triangular crown.

Common beech

Height: 25m (82ft)

You may spot common beeches in woodland or parks. They are tall, with a spreading crown, and their leaves are light-green and oval, turning copper-brown in autumn. The tree has smooth grey bark, and pointed nuts inside hairy husks.

WHEN ....

WHERE ....

Leaves have wavy edges.

The beech nuts are inside hairy husks.

Catkin

The bark peels off in ribbons.

Silver birch

Silver birch

Height: 15m (49ft)

Silver birches are slender trees with silvery bark and drooping branches. They have small, diamond-shaped leaves with double-toothed edges, and catkins in winter. These are long spikes of tiny flowers, also called "lambs' tails".

WHEN ....

WHERE ....

Common lime

Height: 25m (82ft)

Common limes are trees with a broad crown of heart-shaped leaves. The leaves have toothed edges and are hairless beneath. They have yellowish-green, scented flowers in July, and small, round, hard, grey-green fruits hanging from leafy wings.

WHEN _____

WHERE _____

The fruits hang from a leafy wing.

English elm

Height: 30m (98ft)

English elms have become rare in Britain due to disease, and those that remain there do not produce seeds. Tall, with a narrow crown, this tree is often uneven in shape, with rough, oval leaves, and clusters of red flowers. Its seeds (seen in mainland Europe) are transparent and winged, turning brown when ripe.

WHEN _____

WHERE _____

The leaves have double-toothed edges.

Silver lime

Height: 20m (66ft)

This woodland tree has a broad, rounded crown, and rounded leaves that are dark-green above and hairy beneath. Its small, round fruits hang from leafy wings.

WHEN _____

WHERE _____

Pointed leaf tip

Sweet chestnut

Height: 25m (82ft)

Sweet chestnut trees have clusters of edible brown chestnuts in prickly green cases. They are large, tall-crowned trees that have long, narrow leaves with saw-toothed edges. Their bark is sometimes spiral-furrowed.

WHEN _____

WHERE _____

Clusters of two or three fruits containing nuts

15

More trees with simple leaves

Grey alder
Height: 14m (46ft)

Grey alders are fast-growing trees, with catkins and fruit rather like the common alder (see below). They have pointed, oval leaves that are soft and grey underneath, with sharply toothed and lobed edges.

WHEN ....
WHERE ....

Grey alder

Green fruits ripen into brown, woody cones.

Common alder
Height: 12m (39ft)

Common alders often grow near water. They have rounded leaves that fall in late autumn, reddish catkins and fruit like small, brown, woody cones. Their young twigs and leaves are sticky.

WHEN ....
WHERE ....

Common alder

The cone-like fruits stay on all winter.

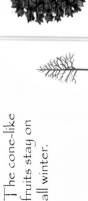

Whitebeam
Height: 8m (26ft)

The flowers and berries of a whitebeam are similar to a rowan's, but they ripen later. You may find this tree growing at the edges of woods. It has large, oval leaves that are white and furry underneath, with toothed edges.

WHEN ....
WHERE ....

WHEN ....
WHERE ....

The leaves are white and furry underneath.

Whitebeam

16

Common pear

Height: 15m (49ft)

Sometimes found in woods and hedgerows, common pears are not really common at all. They are tall, narrow trees, which bear big white flowers in April. The unripe green pears are gritty to eat, but sweet when ripe and golden. The small, dark-green, oval leaves have finely toothed edges and long stalks.

WHEN ....

WHERE ....

The leaves turn red in autumn.

Green pears turn golden when ripe.

Wild cherry

Height: 15m (49ft)

Wild cherry trees bear inedible red cherries, and are covered with a blossom of white flowers in April. Their large, oval leaves turn red in autumn, and have toothed edges and pointed tips. Their bark is reddish-brown and peels in ribbons.

WHEN ....

WHERE ....

The red cherries are not edible.

Crab apple

Height: 10m (33ft)

Crab apples are small, bushy trees found in hedgerows. They have small, rounded leaves with toothed edges and bear pinkish-white flowers in May. The small, speckled reddish-green apples are too sour to eat raw, but can be used in cooking.

WHEN ....

WHERE ....

Sour-tasting apple

Oaks

Oaks are broadleaved trees with simple leaves. Most oaks are deciduous, which means they lose their leaves in winter. They have fruits called acorns.

Sessile oak

Height: 21m (69ft)

It is often hard to tell a sessile oak from an English oak (see below). It has thick, dark-green, long-stalked leaves, tapering to the base, and acorns set close to the twigs. Its branches grow from the stem at different levels and point upwards in a narrow crown.

WHEN ....
WHERE ....

Sessile oak

The acorns are more rounded than those of an English oak.

English oak

Height: 23m (75ft)

An English oak has a broad crown and many large branches growing from the same point. Its trunk is broader and shorter than a sessile oak's, and its leaves grow on much shorter stalks, with ear-like lobes at the base. Its acorns are taller and grow on long stalks.

WHEN ....
WHERE ....

English oak

The acorns are tall and grow on long stalks.

Holm oak

Height: 20m (66ft)

This tree is quite different from other oaks, because it has shiny, evergreen leaves, greyish-green beneath, sometimes with shallow teeth, rather like holly leaves. It is a common ornamental tree, with a broad, dense crown.

WHEN ....
WHERE ....

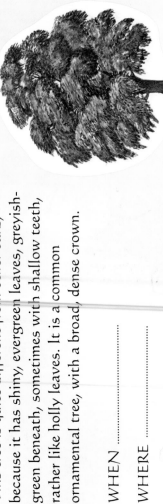

A holm oak's evergreen leaves vary in shape.

Small acorns, almost covered by their cups

18

Red oak

Height: 20m (66ft)

Red oaks have large leaves, with bristly-tipped lobes, that turn reddish-brown in autumn. Their bark is smooth and silvery and they have squat acorns in shallow cups, that ripen in the second year.

WHEN ....
WHERE ....

Red oak

Autumn colour of leaves

Turkey oak

Height: 25m (82ft)

You'll be able to recognize a turkey oak by its stalkless, mossy acorn cups. Its leaves are long and unevenly lobed, and it has whiskers on its buds and at the base of the leaves. The acorns ripen in the second autumn.

WHEN ....
WHERE ....

Turkey oak

The acorn cup is mossy.

Cork oak

Height: 16m (52ft)

This is another evergreen oak. It has shiny leaves with wavy edges. While common in southern Europe, it is extremely rare in Britain. Smaller than other oaks, it has a twisted trunk and branches and thick, corky, whitish bark.

WHEN ....
WHERE ....

The acorns are tiny.

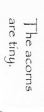

Cork oak

The bark is used for cork.

Poplars

Poplars are broadleaved, deciduous trees with simple leaves. Some bear hanging spikes of flowers called catkins.

Lombardy poplar
Height: 28m (92ft)

You may see this tall, narrow tree growing along roadsides in many parts of Europe. It has furrowed bark, and branches that grow upwards.

WHEN ....

WHERE ....

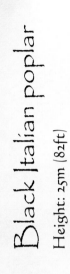

The leaves vary a little in shape.

Lombardy poplar

Black Italian poplar
Height: 25m (82ft)

This poplar is rare in Britain, but you may find it in parks. It is fast-growing, and its trunk and crown often lean away from the wind. It has red catkins, deeply furrowed bark, and dark-green, tear-shaped, pointed leaves, which appear late in spring.

WHEN ....

WHERE ....

Black Italian poplars have fan-shaped crowns.

Leaf from upper branch

Leaf from lower branch

Grey poplar

Grey poplar
Height: 23m (75ft)

The leaves of grey poplars are wavy-edged and downy white underneath, but they vary in shape from the top to the bottom of the tree. The bark is yellowish-grey at the top; dark and furrowed below.

WHEN ....

WHERE ....

20

White poplar
Height: 20m (66ft)

At first glance, it is hard to tell this tree apart from a grey poplar, except that it often leans slightly. If you look closely, the leaf shape is different too: the leaves are five-lobed and downy white below, paler and more rugged nearer the top of the tree. Young trees have diamond shapes on their bark.

WHEN ....

WHERE ....

The leaf stalks are long and flattened.

Aspen

Western balsam poplar
Height: 35m (115ft)

Western balsam poplars takes their name from their sticky, sweet-smelling buds and young leaves. They are tall, fast-growing trees with large, spade-shaped pointed leaves that are paler underneath, white, fluffy seeds and long, purplish catkins.

WHEN ....

WHERE ....

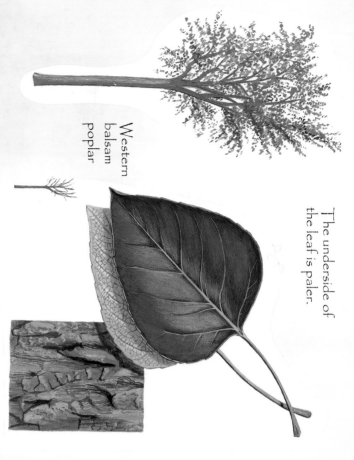

Western balsam poplar

The underside of the leaf is paler.

Aspen
Height: 20m (66ft)

Aspens are smaller than other poplars and often found in woods. They have grey bark with large pores, and rounded, wavy-edged leaves, deep-green on top and paler underneath. The catkins are purplish-grey and fluffy on some trees, white or green and woolly on others.

WHEN ....

WHERE ....

White poplar

Willows

Willow trees belong to the same family as poplars. They all have simple leaves without lobes, and catkins.

The catkins are known as pussy willow.

Goat willow

Height: 7m (23ft)

You may spot a goat willow on damp waste ground. It is a small, bushy tree with broad, rounded, rough grey-green leaves, and silvery-grey, upright catkins in late winter.

WHEN ....

WHERE ....

Goat willow

Female trees have catkins that turn white and fluffy. Male trees have yellow catkins.

White willow

Height: 20m (66ft)

White willows are usually found by streams and rivers. They have long, narrow, finely-toothed leaves, white underneath, and slender twigs that are hard to break. One variety with trailing branches is known as "weeping willow".

WHEN ....

WHERE ....

White willow

Crack willow

Height: 15m (49ft)

This is the most common of the willows. It grows near water and often has its branches cut back to the trunk. Its very long, narrow leaves are bright green above and grey-green below. You can tell it easily from a white willow because its twigs are easy to snap.

WHEN ....

WHERE ....

The crack willow has very long, narrow leaves and catkins.

Trees with lobed leaves

On this page you can see some common trees with lobed leaves. These are simple leaves that are partly divided into sections.

Field maple
Height: 10m (33ft)

Field maples are small round-headed trees, often found in hedges. They have small, dark-green leaves with five lobes, and small, reddish, winged seeds that form a straight line.

WHEN ....

WHERE ....

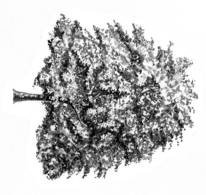

The bobble fruits hang on London plane trees all winter.

Field maple

Reddish winged seeds

Leaves turn golden in autumn.

London plane
Height: 30m (98ft)

Often found in towns, London planes are tall, spreading trees, with spiny "bobble" fruits that hang all winter. Look out for their flaking bark, which leaves yellowish patches on the trunk, and its large, shiny, broad leaves with pointed lobes.

WHEN ....

WHERE ....

The leaves have toothed edges.

Sycamore
Height: 20m (66ft)

Sycamores are large, spreading trees, with smooth, brown bark, becoming scaly. Their leaves are dark-green and leathery, with five lobes. The seeds are winged, in right-angled pairs. See how they twist like propellers, as they fall off the tree.

WHEN ....

WHERE ....

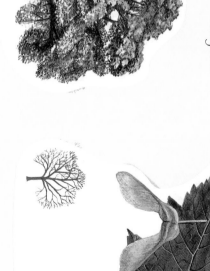

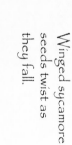

Winged sycamore seeds twist as they fall.

23

Compound leaves

All the trees on these two pages are broadleaved, with compound leaves. This means they are made up of smaller leaflets.

Common ash

Height: 25m (82ft)

Seen in woods, hedgerows or open hillsides, this tree has pale-grey bark and compound leaves with nine to thirteen leaflets. Its leaves come out in late spring, after purplish flowers. Seed clusters hang on the tree into winter.

WHEN ....

WHERE ....

The seeds grow in clusters, and the buds are black.

Common ash

Fruit

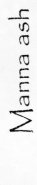

Manna ash

Height: 20m (66ft)

Manna ashes are named after the sugary liquid known as manna that oozes from their smooth, grey bark. They have compound leaves of five to nine stalked leaflets and clusters of white flowers in May. They are most common in woodland.

WHEN ....

WHERE ....

One flower from a cluster

Manna ash

The leaflets are downy near the veins.

Rowan

Height: 7m (23ft)

Rowans, or mountain ashes, are small trees, not related to the other ashes, and often found alone on mountainsides. They have small, toothed, compound leaves, clusters of creamy-white flowers in May, and red berries in August.

WHEN ....

WHERE ....

Rowan

24

Common walnut

Height: 15m (49ft)

Common walnuts are broad-crowned trees, with edible walnuts inside smooth, green cases. The bark is fairly smooth and grey, with some deep cracks. Their leaves have seven to nine toothed leaflets, and hollow, chambered twigs.

WHERE ....

WHEN ....

The leaves are pinkish when they first open, turning green later.

Common walnut

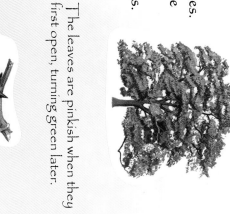

Smooth, green case containing edible walnut

The leaflets have smooth edges.

False acacia

False acacia

Height: 20m (66ft)

False acacias usually grow in dry, sandy soil. They have hanging clusters of white flowers in June, and seeds in pods. The bark is deeply furrowed, and the delicate leaves are made up of many small leaflets. The tree has pairs of sharp thorns on its twigs and often has several trunks.

WHEN ....

WHERE ....

Horse chestnut

Height: 25m (82ft)

This tree is common in parks and avenues, and is famous for its brown, inedible "conkers" in green, spiny cases. It has compound leaves made up of five to seven large leaflets, and upright "candles" of white or pink flowers in May.

WHEN ....

WHERE ....

Conker

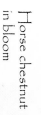

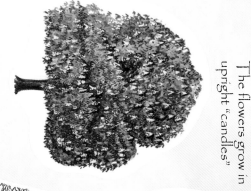

Horse chestnut in bloom

The flowers grow in upright "candles"

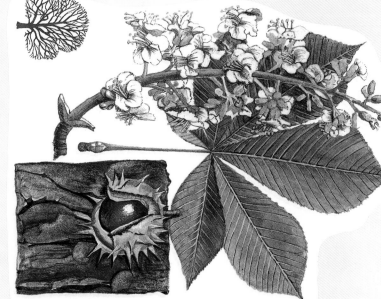

Unusual trees

Here is a selection of very distinctive trees to look out for. Some of them you will only find in gardens and parks.

Ripe fruit

Unripe fruit

Black mulberry
Height: 15m (49ft)

Black mulberries are low, broad-crowned ornamental trees, with short trunks and twisted branches. They have rough, heart-shaped leaves with toothed edges, short, spiked flowers and edible blackish-red berries.

In old trees, the branches grow right to the ground, and sometimes lean over.

WHEN ....

WHERE ....

Grey, scaly bark which flakes off in "plates"

European fan palm
Height: 4m (13ft)

European fan palms likes dry, sunny conditions and are rare in Britain. They have large, fan-shaped leaves, made up of 12–15 stiff, pointed leaflets, and large clusters of small flowers and fruits. In the wild, the plants form trunkless clumps of leaves.

WHEN ....

WHERE ....

The tall trunk only exists in planted palms.

Holly
Height: 10m (33ft)

Holly is easy to spot. It is a small tree or bush, with smooth, grey-green bark, and shiny, dark, evergreen leaves with thorny prickles. It has small white flowers, and poisonous red berries in autumn and winter.

The berries only appear on some trees.

WHEN ....

WHERE ....

26

Tulip tree

Height: 20m (66ft)

Tulip trees takes their name from the large, tulip-like flowers that come out in June. They are tall and narrow-crowned, with smooth, four-lobed leaves that turn golden in autumn, and upright, brown, cone-like fruits.

WHEN ....

WHERE ....

Tulip-like flower

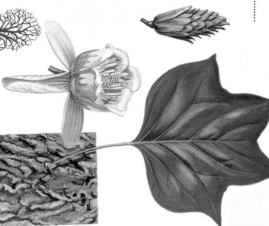

Coast redwood

Height: 35–110m (115–360ft)

In its natural home of California, this tall tree can grow taller than any other. It has thick, spongy, reddish bark, small, round cones and hard, sharp-pointed needles that are dark green above and white-banded below.

WHEN ....

WHERE ....

The needles are parted on either side of the twig.

Monkey puzzle

Height: 23m (75ft)

Also called Chile pines, monkey puzzles are strange-looking trees, with wrinkled bark and twisting branches. They have a broad, round crown and a pole-like trunk. Their stiff, leathery leaves have sharp points, and grow all around the shoots.

WHEN ....

WHERE ....

The leaves overlap each other.

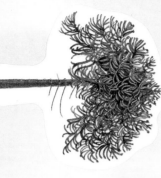

Maidenhair

Height: 23m (75ft)

Also called ginkgos, maidenhairs are neither conifers nor broadleaved trees, but are in a group of their own. They are tall and slender, with double-lobed, fan-shaped leaves with a deep cleft, that turn bright yellow in autumn. Some trees have hanging fruits, like small plums.

WHEN ....

WHERE ....

The fruit looks like a small plum.

Trees checklist

This list will help you find every tree in the book. The first number after each tree tells you which page it is on. The second number (in brackets) shows the number of the stickers.

Aspen 21 (19)
Atlas cedar 10 (1)
Black Italian poplar 20 (15)
Black mulberry 26 (2)
Cedar of Lebanon 10 (33)
Chile pine (see Monkey puzzle)
Coast redwood 27 (18)
Common alder 16 (47)
Common ash 24 (49)
Common beech 14 (68)
Common lime 15 (67)
Common pear 17 (37)
Common walnut 25 (56)
Cork oak 19 (7)
Corsican pine 6 (63)
Crab apple 17 (10)
Crack willow 22 (51)
Dawn redwood 13 (35)
Deodar cedar 10 (30)
Douglas fir 9 (64)
English elm 15 (54)
English oak 18 (61)
European fan palm 26 (26)
European larch 11 (13)

European silver fir 8 (65)
False acacia 25 (55)
Field maple 23 (52)
Giant sequoia 13 (29)
Goat willow 22 (28)
Grey alder 16 (44)
Grey poplar 20 (25)
Holly 26 (41)
Holm oak 18 (39)
Horse chestnut 25 (16)
Japanese larch 11 (8)
Japanese red cedar 11 (38)
Juniper 12 (34)
Lombardy poplar 20 (20)
London plane 23 (50)
Maidenhair 27 (42)
Manna ash 24 (36)
Maritime pine 7 (11)
Monkey puzzle 27 (48)
Monterey cypress 12 (24)
Monterey pine 7 (62)
Noble fir 9 (4)
Norway spruce 8 (53)
Red oak 19 (31)

Rowan 24 (27)
Scots pine 6 (9)
Sessile oak 18 (57)
Shore pine 6 (60)
Sierra redwood (see Giant sequoia)
Silver birch 14 (32)
Silver lime 15 (69)
Sitka spruce 8 (5)
Southern beech 14 (66)
Swamp cypress 13 (40)
Sweet chestnut 15 (23)
Swiss stone pine 7 (17)
Sycamore 23 (3)
Tulip tree 27 (45)
Turkey oak 19 (58)
Wellingtonia (see Giant sequoia)
Western balsam poplar 21 (59)
Western hemlock 9 (12)
Western red cedar 12 (22)
Whitebeam 16 (46)
White poplar 21 (14)
White willow 22 (21)
Wild cherry 17 (43)
Yew 9 (6)

Tree words

Bract – on some cones, a leaf-like part that grows at the base of each scale

Broadleaved – a tree with wide, flat leaves. Most broadleaved trees are deciduous.

Bud – a swelling on a branch that grows into leaf-shoots or flowers

Compound leaf – a type of leaf that is divided into smaller "leaflets"

Conifer – a tree that bears cones containing its seeds. Most conifers are evergreen with needle-like leaves.

Crown – the leaves and branches at the top of a tree

Deciduous – a tree that sheds all its leaves every year at the end of the growing season

Evergreen – a tree that is covered with leaves all year round

Fruit – part of a tree that holds its seeds. It may take many forms, including berries, nuts, cones and winged seeds.

Hardwood – a name sometimes used for broadleaved trees

Leaflet – a section of a compound leaf

Lobed leaf – a type of simple leaf. Its partly divided sections have round edges.

Sapling – a young tree, over 1m (3¼ft) high, with a trunk up to 7cm (2¾in) around

Seedling – a newly sprouted tree, under 1m (3¼ft) high

Simple leaf – a type of leaf that is all in one piece

Softwood – a name sometimes used for conifers

Toothed leaf – a type of leaf with jagged edges

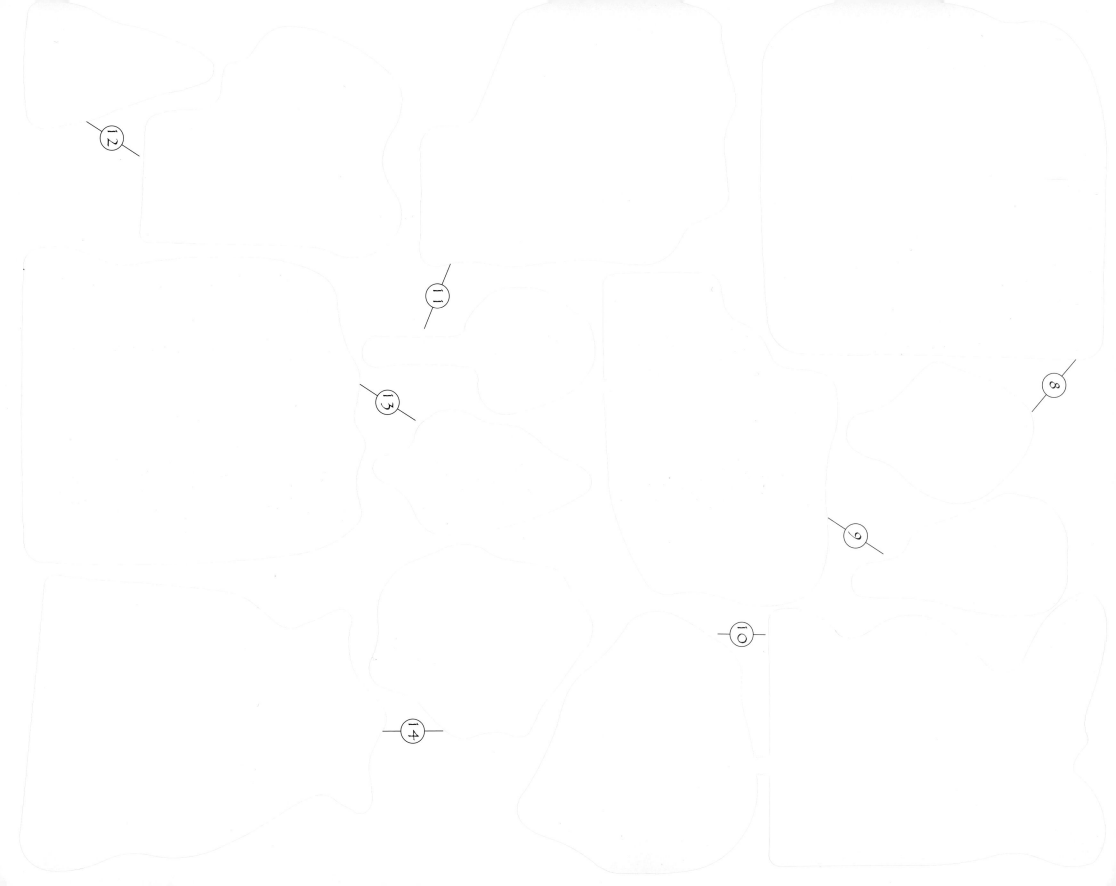

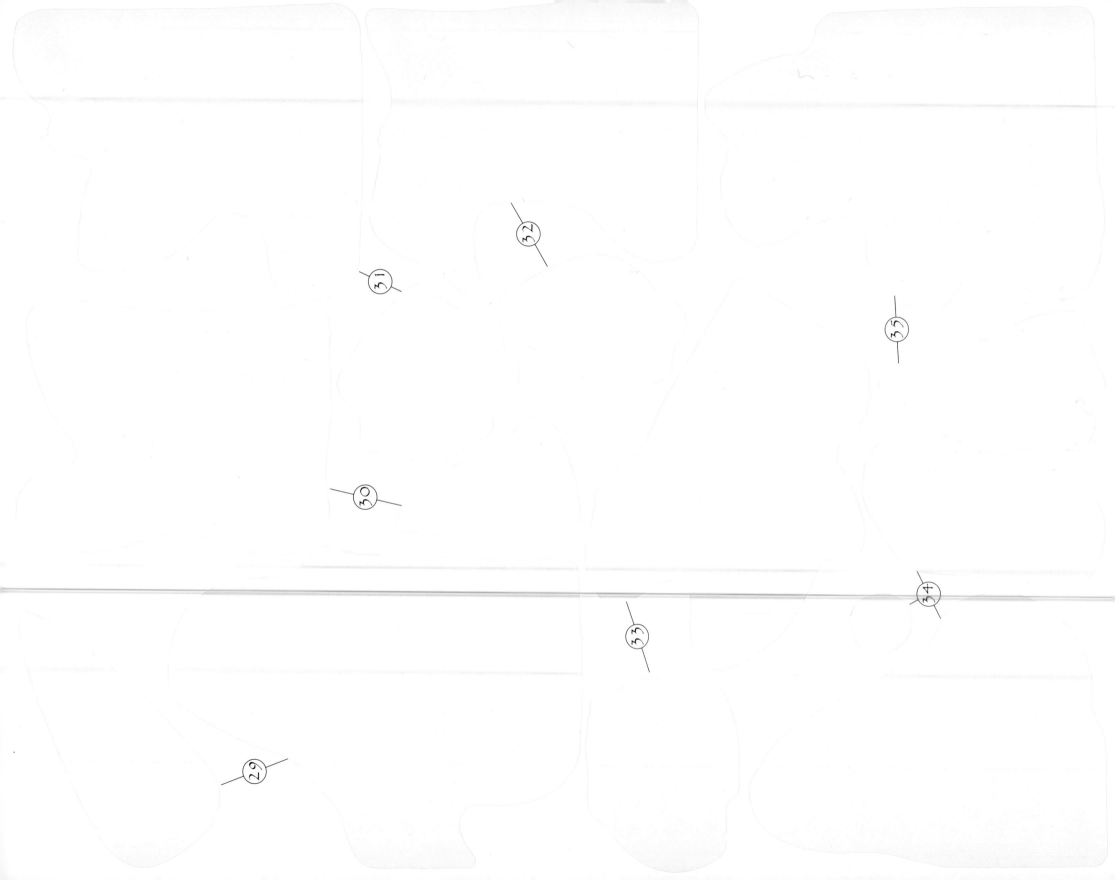

36

40

38

41

39

42

37

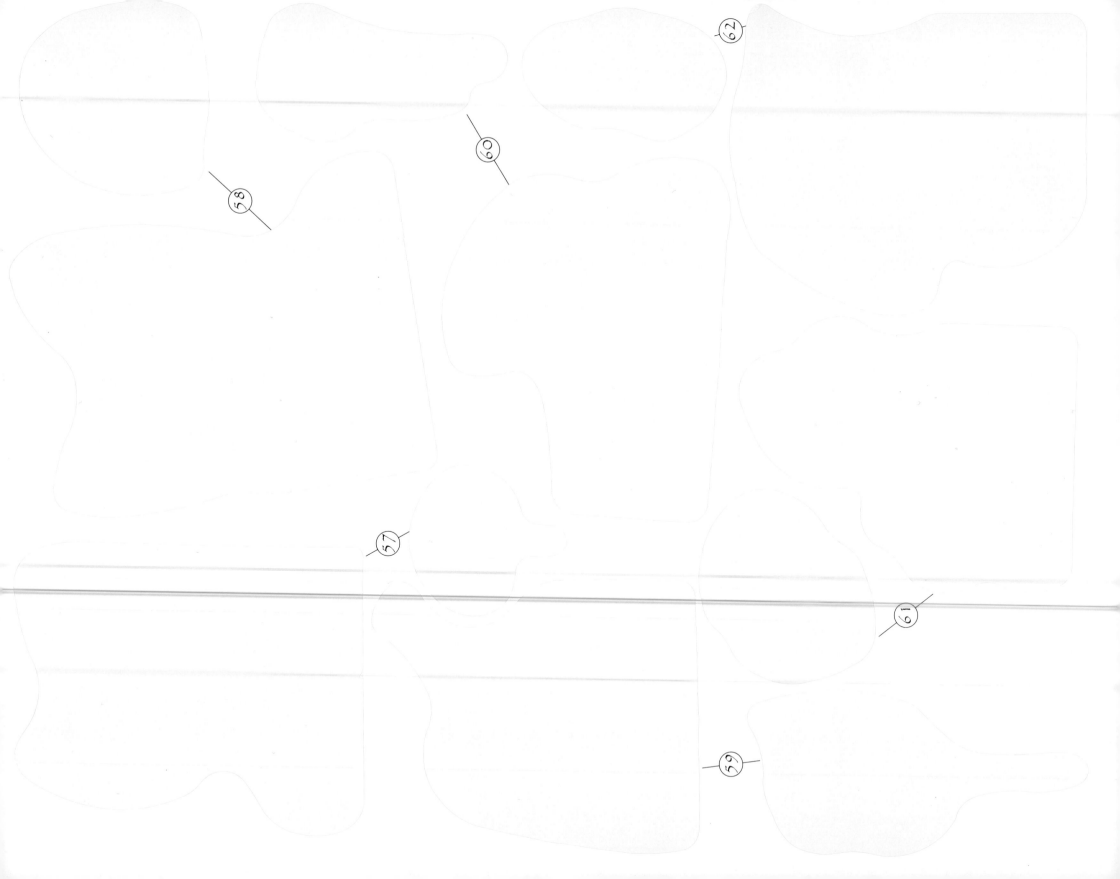

Birds

Here are some of the words used to describe parts of a bird.

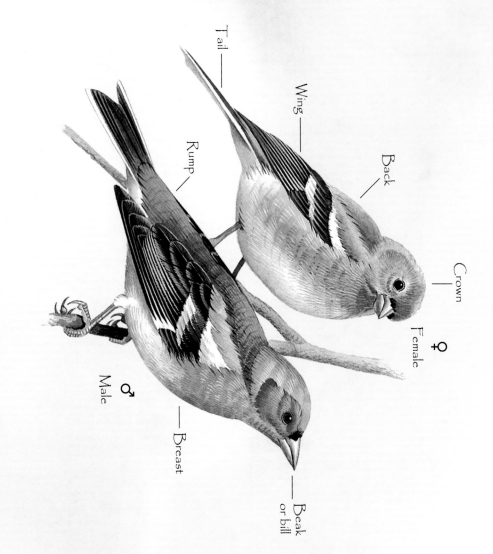

Tail

Wing

Back

Rump

Crown

Female ♀

Male ♂

Breast

Beak
or bill

Seabirds

Gannet

Gannet

Length: 92cm (36¼in)

Adult gannets are white with creamy-yellow heads and black wingtips. They spend most of their lives at sea and plunge into the water to catch fish.

WHEN ....

WHERE ....

Razorbill

Length: 41cm (16in)

Razorbills are black with white breasts. They have large bills with flat sides. Groups of razorbills nest on cliffs and spend the winter out at sea.

WHEN ....

WHERE ....

Neck and throat are white in winter

Razorbill (summer)

Guillemot

Length: 42cm (16½in)

Guillemots (pronounced "gilli-mots") are black with a white breast. They look similar to razorbills, but have thinner, more pointed beaks.

WHEN ....

WHERE ....

Neck and throat are white in winter

Guillemot (summer)

Puffin

Length: 30cm (12in)

Puffins are fairly small seabirds that nests in holes in cliffs and rocky islands. They are black with white faces and breasts. In the summer they have stripy bills and red legs.

WHEN ....

WHERE ....

Puffin (summer)

Fulmar

Length: 47cm (18½in)

This greyish-white seabird nests on cliffs by the sea and often flies close to the waves. It has a fat bill.

WHEN ....

WHERE ....

Fulmar

Black-headed
gull (summer)

Black-headed
gull (winter)

Great black-backed gull

Length: 66cm (26in)

This large gull is white with a black back and wings. It has pale pink legs and a bright yellow bill with a red spot.

WHEN _____

WHERE _____

Black-headed gull

Length: 37cm (14½in)

This gull has grey wings and a white body with a red bill and legs. Its face is dark brown in the summer.

WHEN _____

WHERE _____

Herring gull

Herring gull

Length: 56cm (22in)

This seaside gull is white with a light-grey back and black and white wingtips. Its bill is yellow with a red spot and its legs are pink.

WHEN _____

WHERE _____

Common gull

Great black-
backed gull

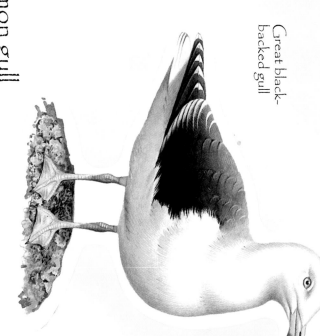

Common gull

Length: 41cm (16in)

You may see this gull far from the sea. It is grey and white, with a yellow bill and legs, and black and white wingtips.

WHEN _____

WHERE _____

31

Ducks

Mallard

Length: 58cm (23in)

Mallards are common on inland waters, such as lakes and ponds. The female is speckled brown all over. Males have a light-grey and brown body, with a glossy, dark-green head and a yellow bill.

WHEN ....

WHERE ....

♀

♂

Mallard

Shoveler

Length: 51cm (20in)

This duck is easy to spot because of its long, wide bill. The female is speckled brown. The male has a brilliant white breast and a glossy green head.

WHEN ....

WHERE ....

♀

♂

Shoveler

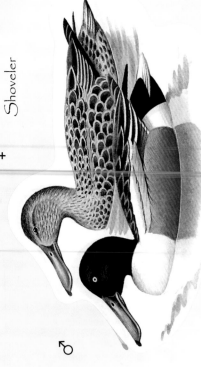

Teal

Length: 35cm (13¾in)

This very shy creature is the smallest European duck. The female is speckled brown. The male has a speckled breast, a grey body and a colourful head with green and reddish-brown markings.

WHEN ....

WHERE ....

♂

♀

Teal

Pochard

Length: 46cm (18in)

Pochards (pronounced "poach-ards") are often seen in winter. The male has a reddish-brown head, black neck and pale grey body. The female is a plain light brown. Both sexes have dark tails and grey bills.

WHEN ....

WHERE ....

♂

♀

Pochard

Wigeon

Length: 46cm (18in)

Wigeons sometimes graze in fields. The females are brown. Males have grey bodies with black tails, and reddish-brown heads with a yellow stripe on top.

WHEN ....

WHERE ....

♂

♀

Wigeon

Eider

Length: 58cm (23in)

Eider ducks are found on rocky seashores. The males are black and white with a lime-green ear patch. The females are brown with narrow stripes. Eiders are some of the fastest-flying of all birds.

WHEN ....

WHERE ....

Eider

♂

♀

Tufted duck

Length: 43cm (17in)

Tufted ducks have a drooping tuft on the backs of their heads, but the male's tuft is longer. He has a black body with a bright white side patch. The female is dark brown. Both have bright yellow eyes.

WHEN ....

WHERE ....

Tufted duck

♀

♂

Red-breasted merganser

Length: 58cm (23in)

This duck is often seen near the sea. The male has a green head, a spotted brown breast and a black and white body. The female is grey with a brown head. Both have ruffled, tufted feathers on the backs of their heads.

WHEN ....

WHERE ....

Red-breasted merganser

♂

♀

Goldeneye

Length: 46cm (18in)

Both male and female goldeneyes have yellow eyes and big heads. The female is speckled grey with a brown head, and the male is black and white, with a white circle on his face.

WHEN ....

WHERE ....

Goldeneye

♀

♂

Goosander

Length: 66cm (26in)

Both the male and the female have pointed, red beaks. The female is brown and grey, with a shaggy crest on the back of her head. The male has a black and white body and a green head with no crest.

WHEN ....

WHERE ....

Goosander

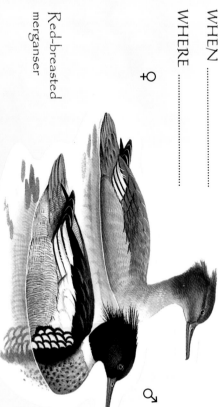

♀

♂

33

More waders

Golden plover

Golden plover
(northern Europe)

Length: 28cm (11in)

This plover has a bright golden-brown, speckled back. In summer, its face and underside are black, with white edges. Its legs are grey.

WHEN ....

WHERE ....

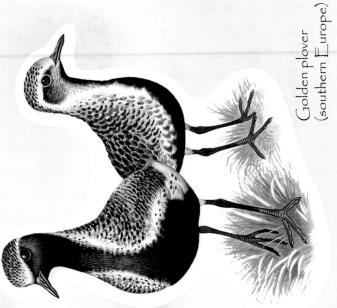

Golden plover
(southern Europe)

Whimbrel

Length: 40cm (15¾in)

A whimbrel looks like a small curlew, but its beak is shorter, and it has black stripes on its head. Like a curlew, it is sometimes found at the seaside.

WHEN ....

WHERE ....

Bar-tailed godwit

Length: 37cm (14½in)

When it flies, a bar-tailed godwit shows its white tail, which has dark brown stripes running across it. The rest of its body is spotted brown and it has a long, slightly upward-curving bill.

WHEN ....

WHERE ....

Whimbrel

Bar-tailed
godwit

Dunlin

Length: 19cm (7½in)

Dunlins can be seen at the seaside, and sometimes on moors in spring. They are small waders with brown or grey backs. They have black bellies in summer.

WHEN ....

WHERE ....

Dunlin (winter)

Dunlin (summer)

38

Avocet

Length: 43cm (17in)

This large wader usually lives near the sea. It is white, with striking black markings on its back and head. It has long, blue-grey legs, and an unusual bill that curves upwards.

WHEN ....

WHERE ....

Woodcock

Woodcock

Length: 34cm (13½in)

Woodcocks are shy and live in damp woodlands. Their feathers are patterned dark and light brown all over. The pattern helps them to hide in the leaves on the woodland floor, where they make their nests.

WHEN ....

WHERE ....

Avocet

Sanderling

Length: 20cm (8in)

Sanderlings can be seen running around on sandy beaches, catching small creatures washed up by the tide. In winter, they have white bellies and speckled grey backs.

WHEN ....

WHERE ....

Snipe

Snipe

Length: 27cm (10¾in)

This bird lives in marshy areas and bogs. It is speckled brown, with brown and white feathers on its back. It has a very long beak.

WHEN ....

WHERE ....

Sanderling (winter)

Owls

Short-eared owl

Length: 37cm (14½in)

This owl has two little "ear-tufts" on its head: they are not ears, but feathers. It has large, yellow eyes and big, feathered feet.

WHEN ....

WHERE ....

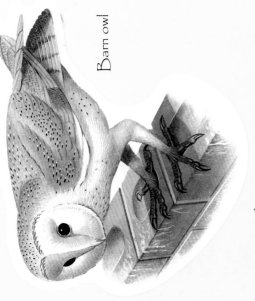

Short-eared owl

Long-eared owl

Length: 34cm (13½in)

This owl has two large ear-tufts on top of its head. Its body is long and thin, and its feathers are speckled brown.

WHEN ....

WHERE ....

Long-eared owl

Barn owl

Length: 34cm (13½in)

Barn owls have a long, screeching call. Their breast feathers are speckled white; those on their backs are golden-brown. They have big feet and big, white, heart-shaped faces.

WHEN ....

WHERE ....

Barn owl

Tawny owl

Length: 38cm (15in)

This large owl lives in woods. It is speckled light and dark brown, and has big, black eyes. The tawny owl is plump-looking, with a large, round head. Its call is "tu-wit, tu-woo".

WHEN ....

WHERE ....

Tawny owl

Little owl

Length: 22cm (8¾in)

A small, flat-headed owl that flies over farmland and hunts at dusk. It nests in tree-holes. It may often be seen perching in daytime, bobbing its head up and down when curious.

WHEN ....

WHERE ....

Little owl

Wagtails

Pied wagtail and white wagtail

Length: 18cm (7in)

Pied wagtails are common in Britain, and white wagtails are more often seen in Europe. Wagtails are named for their habit of always wagging their tails up and down.

WHEN ....

WHERE ....

White wagtail

Pied wagtail

Grey wagtail

Length: 18cm (7in)

Grey wagtails are, in fact, quite brightly coloured. They have yellow feathers on the breast and underside. The male has a black patch under his chin.

WHEN ....

WHERE ....

Grey wagtail

Woodpeckers

Green woodpecker

Length: 32cm (12½in)

Green woodpeckers are quite common in woods and parks. They have green wings and backs, with paler underparts, a yellow rump, a red "cap", and red and black face-markings. Their call sounds like a loud laugh.

WHEN ....

WHERE ....

♂

Green woodpecker

Great spotted woodpecker

Length: 23cm (9in)

This woodpecker can sometimes be heard drumming on trees in spring. It has a white breast and a black and white body, with red marks under its tail. The male has a red patch on the back of its head.

WHEN ....

WHERE ....

Great spotted woodpecker

♂

Lesser spotted woodpecker

Lesser spotted woodpecker

Length: 14cm (5½in)

This little woodpecker is striped black and white, with a short tail. The male has a bright red crown.

WHEN ....

WHERE ....

Warblers

Reed warbler

Reed warbler

Length: 13cm (5in)

This bird lives in wet places. It is plain brown with a paler underside and a reddish-brown tail. Its eyes are black and its legs are short and brown.

WHEN ....

WHERE ....

Blackcap

Length: 14cm (5½in)

Blackcaps are seen in wooded areas, moving from perch to perch as they sing. The males have a black "cap" on their heads. The female's is reddish-brown.

WHEN ....

WHERE ....

♀

♂

Blackcap

Willow warbler

Willow warbler

Length: 11cm (4¼in)

This is a small, very common warbler. Its feathers are greenish-gold. It has a darker stripe across its eye. Its song is a sweet trill.

WHEN ....

WHERE ....

Sedge warbler

Sedge warbler

Length: 13cm (5in)

This warbler nests in thick trees and bushes near water. It is mostly brown, with darker brown stripes on its wings and a creamy-white breast. It has a white stripe above each eye.

WHEN ....

WHERE ....

♂

Whitethroat

Whitethroat

Length: 14cm (5½in)

Whitethroats hide in thick bushes. They have white undersides and throats and slightly stripy reddish-brown backs. The male has a grey head.

WHEN ....

WHERE ....

Finches

Chaffinch

Length: 15cm (6in)

Chaffinches are often seen in gardens. The male is brightly coloured, with a pink breast and face, a grey head and two white bars on its wings. The female is less colourful, but can still be identified by her white bars.

WHEN ....

WHERE ....

Chaffinch

♀

♂

Goldfinch

Length: 12cm (4¾in)

This little finch is brown, with a red, white and black face and a yellow bar on its wings. It is often found in weedy places.

WHEN ....

WHERE ....

Goldfinch

Bullfinch

Length: 15cm (6in)

Bullfinches have rounded bodies and large heads with black faces and caps. Their wings are grey and black with a white stripe. The male has a pink breast; the female's is brown.

WHEN ....

WHERE ....

Bullfinch

♂

♀

♀

Greenfinch

Length: 15cm (6in)

Greenfinches are yellowish-green, with grey and yellow markings on their wings and tails. The males are more brightly coloured than the females.

WHEN ....

WHERE ....

Greenfinch

♂

Crossbill

Length: 16cm (6¼in)

Crossbills use their crossed-over bills to break seeds out of pine cones. The male crossbill is reddish-brown with dark wings, and the female is a light-green colour.

WHEN ....

WHERE ....

Crossbill

45

Birds of prey

Golden eagle

Golden eagle

Length: 83cm (32¾in)

This large bird of prey hunts small animals. It is a brown colour all over, with yellow feet and a short, strong, yellow beak. Its wings are long and broad.

WHEN ....
WHERE ....

Buzzard

Buzzard

Length: 54cm (21¼in)

This bird has wide, rounded wings with pale patches on them, and no dark bars on its tail. Its feathers are brown and its feet yellow.

WHEN ....
WHERE ....

Sparrowhawk

Sparrowhawk

♂

Length: Female 38cm (15in), Male 30cm (12in)

Sparrowhawks hunt other birds. The male has a bluish-grey back and wings, and a striped underside. Its grey tail has four or five dark bars. The female is larger and browner in colour. Both have yellow feet.

WHEN ....
WHERE ....

Other birds

Dunnock

Dunnock

Length: 14.5cm (5¾in)

This common bird often visits gardens. It has a brown, stripy back and a paler underside. Its head and neck are bluish-grey. It has a short beak and large feet.

WHEN ....
WHERE ....

Skylark

Skylark

Length: 18cm (7in)

Skylarks live in fields and farmland. They have streaky brown feathers, and a small crest on their heads, which they raise when excited.

WHEN ....
WHERE ....

Swift

Length: 17cm (6¾in)

Swifts are often found in small flocks and are fast, skilful fliers, even able to sleep in the air. They are dark brown, with short necks and short, forked tails. Their wings are very long and pointed.

WHEN ....

WHERE ....

Swift

House martin

Length: 13cm (5in)

House martins are small and dark blue with a large, white patch across the rump. They are snow-white underneath, and have short, forked tails.

WHEN ....

WHERE ....

House martin

Swallow

Length: 19cm (7½in)

Swallows have very long, forked tails. They have blue-black backs with red markings on their faces, and are white underneath.

WHEN ....

WHERE ....

Swallow

Kingfisher

Length: 17cm (6¾in)

This brilliantly coloured bird lives near lakes and rivers. It has bright blue-green wings and an orange breast. It has patches of white on its face, and a long bill.

WHEN ....

WHERE ....

Kingfisher

Nightjar

Length: 27cm (10¾in)

Nightjars hunt insects on summer nights. They rest on the ground by day, where their patterned, bark-like feathers make them very hard to spot.

WHEN ....

WHERE ....

Nightjar

Other birds

Waxwing

Length: 17cm (6¾in)

This unusual-looking bird may be seen in winter.
It is reddish-brown, with black, red and white
marks on its wingtips, tail and face. It has
a large, reddish-brown crest on its head.

WHEN ....
WHERE ....

Waxwing

Cuckoo

Length: 30cm (12in)

This bird's "cuckoo" song is a common sound in the
countryside in summer. The cuckoo is grey, with a
black and white striped breast and a very large, grey,
stripy tail. It has a short bill, and is well-known for
laying its eggs in the nests of other birds.

WHEN ....
WHERE ....

House
sparrow

♂

House sparrow

Length: 17cm (6¾in)

House sparrows are still common in Europe,
and are often seen near houses, though not
as often as they once were. They are
black and brown with a paler underside.
The male has a black face and throat.

WHEN ....

WHERE ....

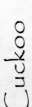

Dipper

Dipper

Length: 18cm (7in)

Dippers live near fast-flowing streams
and dive underwater to find food. They are
dark brown and black, with a white throat
and breast and a reddish-brown underside.

WHEN ....
WHERE ....

Cuckoo

♀

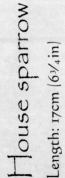

Great grey shrike

Length: 24cm (9½in)

This uncommon bird has a light-grey breast and
a dark back. It has black and white marks on its
wings and a black band across its face. It has
a thick, strong, black bill and a long, grey tail.

WHEN ....
WHERE ....

Great grey
shrike

Goldcrest

Length: 9cm (3½in)

Goldcrests are the smallest birds in Europe. They have round bodies and short necks, and their feathers are greenish-grey, with white stripes on the wings. They have a bright yellow stripe on their crowns.

WHEN ....

WHERE ....

Hoopoe

Goldcrest

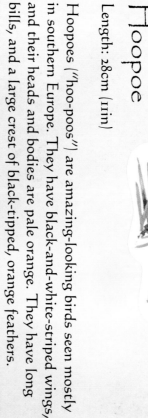

Hoopoe

Length: 28cm (11in)

Hoopoes ("hoo-poos") are amazing-looking birds seen mostly in southern Europe. They have black-and-white-striped wings, and their heads and bodies are pale orange. They have long bills, and a large crest of black-tipped, orange feathers.

WHEN ....

WHERE ....

Robin

Length: 14cm (5½in)

Robins are very common in woods and gardens. They have bright red breasts, and brown wings and backs.

WHEN ....

WHERE ....

Robin

Wren

Wren

Length: 9.5cm (3¾in)

This tiny bird is common and has a loud song. It has a short, round body, short wings and a pointed beak. Its feathers are speckled brown.

WHEN ....

WHERE ....

Treecreeper

Length: 13cm (5in)

This bird climbs tree trunks looking for insects to eat. It is brown and white, with a short, curved beak and a rather long tail.

WHEN ....

WHERE ....

Treecreeper

51

Birds checklist

This list will help you find every bird in the book. The first number after each bird tells you which page it is on. The second number (in brackets) is the number of the sticker.

Avocet 39 (97)
Barn owl 40 (61)
Bar-tailed godwit 38 (78)
Black grouse 42 (64)
Blackbird 46 (98)
Blackcap 44 (48)
Black-headed gull 31 (66)
Blue tit 47 (47)
Bullfinch 45 (26)
Buzzard 48 (24)
Canada goose 34 (69)
Capercaillie 42 (32)
Carrion and hooded crows 43 (79)
Chaffinch 45 (72)
Coal tit 47 (83)
Common gull 31 (17)
Common sandpiper 37 (38)
Coot 35 (39)
Crested tit 47 (34)
Crossbill 45 (85)
Cuckoo 50 (35)
Curlew 37 (71)
Dipper 50 (25)
Dunlin 38 (7)
Dunnock 48 (89)
Eider 33 (30)
Fieldfare 46 (95)
Fulmar 30 (92)
Gannet 30 (23)
Goldcrest 51 (94)
Golden eagle 48 (99)
Golden plover 38 (6)
Goldeneye 33 (100)
Goldfinch 45 (52)

Goosander 33 (45)
Great black-backed gull 31 (81)
Great grey shrike 50 (41)
Great spotted woodpecker 41 (11)
Great tit 47 (56)
Green woodpecker 41 (57)
Greenfinch 45 (21)
Grey heron 34 (62)
Grey wagtail 41 (19)
Greylag goose 34 (101)
Guillemot 30 (68)
Herring gull 31 (96)
Hoopoe 51 (20)
House martin 49 (2)
House sparrow 50 (51)
Kingfisher 49 (59)
Knot 37 (60)
Lapwing 36 (73)
Lesser spotted woodpecker 41 (33)
Little owl 40 (86)
Long-eared owl 40 (50)
Magpie 43 (46)
Mallard 32 (58)
Moorhen 35 (53)
Mute swan 34 (36)
Nightjar 49 (55)
Nuthatch 47 (22)
Oystercatcher 36 (82)
Pheasant 42 (87)
Pied and white wagtails 41 (16)
Pochard 32 (1)
Ptarmigan 42 (42)
Puffin 30 (10)
Raven 43 (70)

Razorbill 30 (9)
Red-breasted merganser 33 (5)
Redshank 37 (40)
Redwing 46 (88)
Reed warbler 44 (102)
Ringed plover 37 (49)
Robin 51 (67)
Rock dove 35 (75)
Rook 43 (84)
Ruff 36 (37)
Sanderling 39 (76)
Sedge warbler 44 (74)
Short-eared owl 40 (4)
Shoveler 32 (43)
Skylark 48 (77)
Snipe 39 (14)
Song thrush 46 (63)
Sparrowhawk 48 (3)
Starling 46 (54)
Swallow 49 (93)
Swift 49 (12)
Tawny owl 40 (18)
Teal 32 (65)
Treecreeper 51 (44)
Tufted duck 33 (13)
Turnstone 36 (28)
Waxwing 50 (15)
Whimbrel 38 (27)
Whitethroat 44 (8)
Wigeon 32 (29)
Willow warbler 44 (31)
Woodcock 39 (90)
Woodpigeon 35 (80)
Wren 51 (91)

11

12

13

14

15

16

17

18

19

20

21

22

23

24

25

26

27

28

29

30

35

37

32

33

36

38

31

39

34

42

44

49

46

41

48

47

45

40

43

50

51

52

53

54

55

56

57

58

59

60

61

62

63

64

65

66

67

68

69

70

78

76

74

71

75

77

72

79

73

80

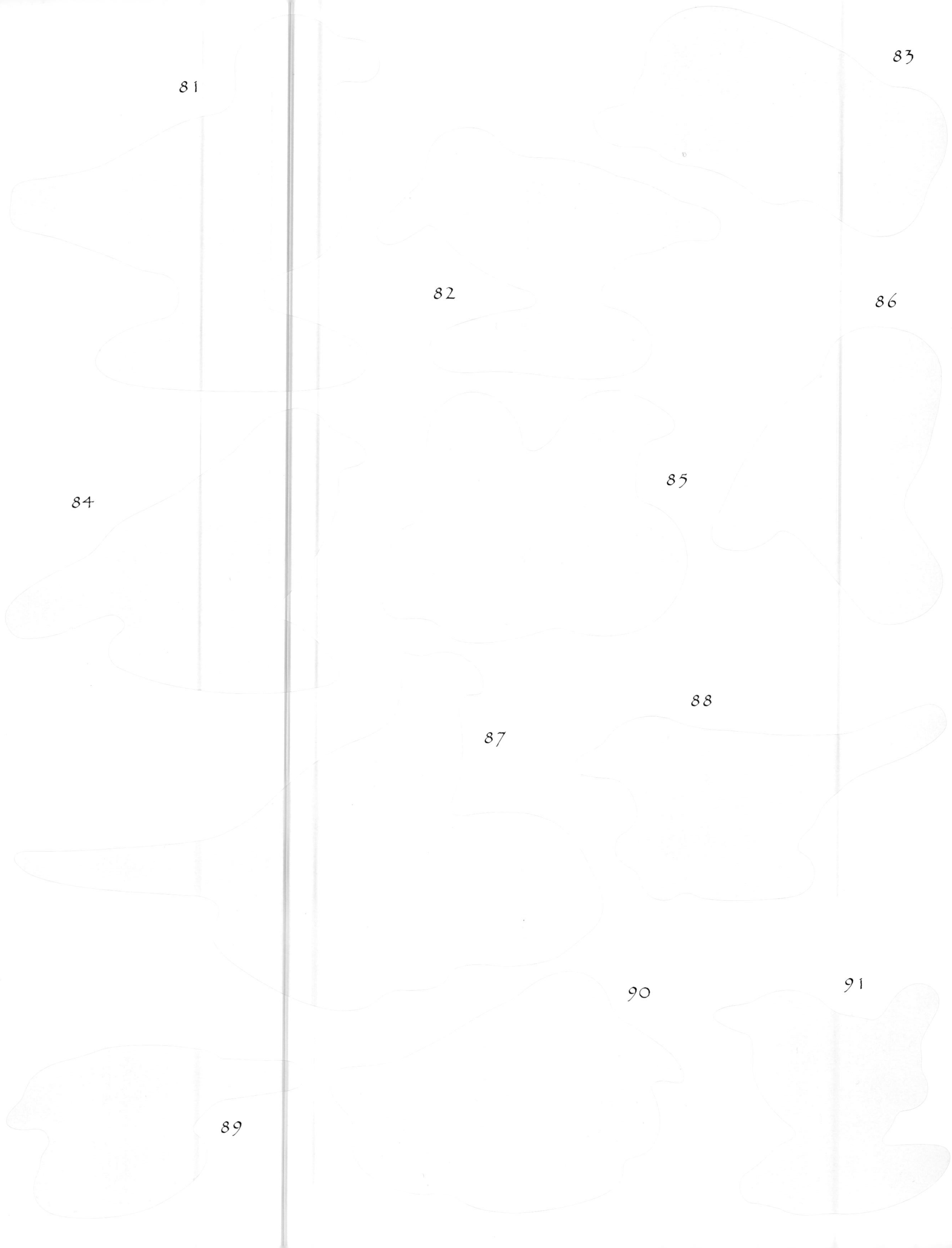

81

82

83

84

85

86

87

88

89

90

91

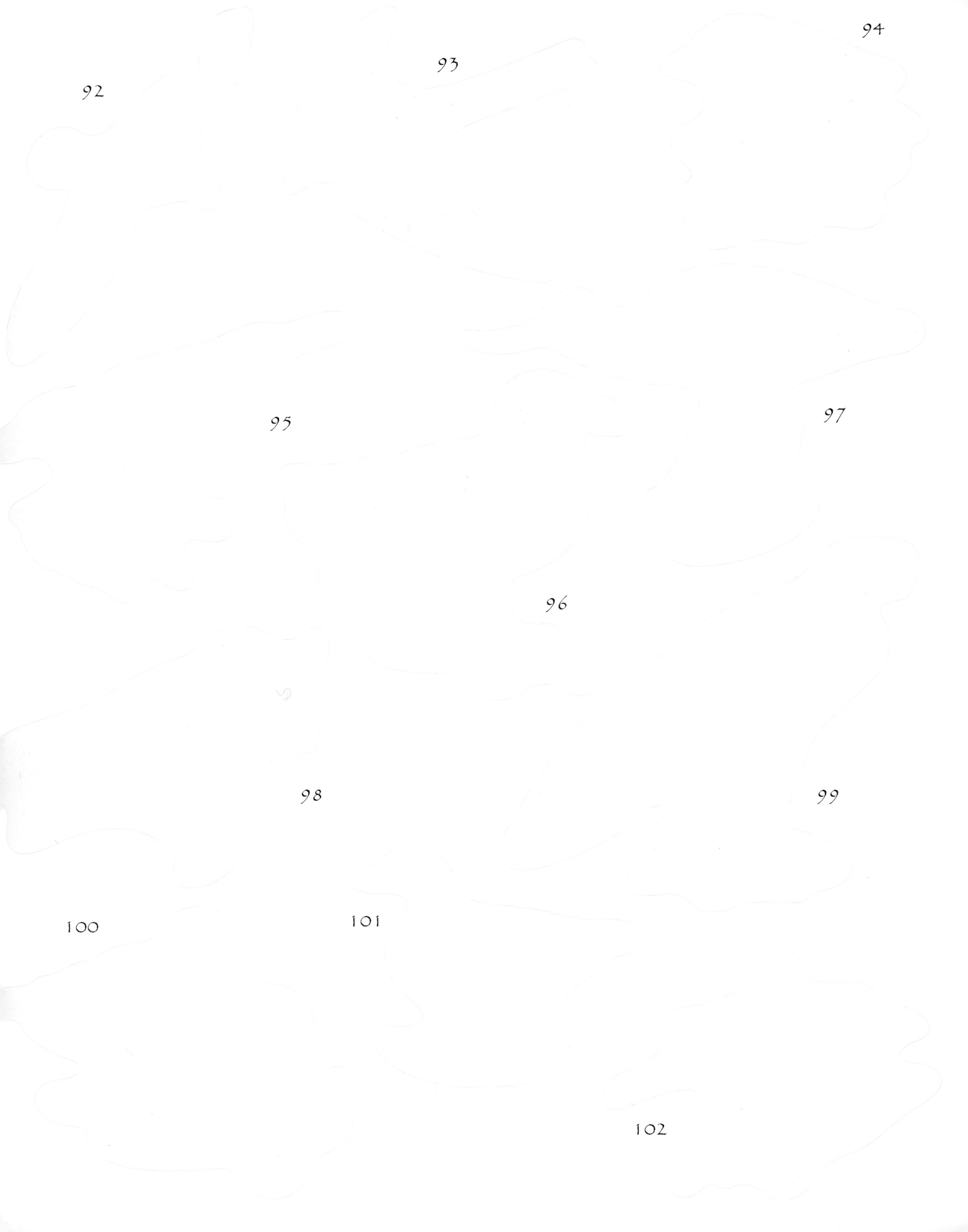

92

93

94

95

96

97

98

99

100

101

102

Flowers

Here are some of the words used to describe parts of a flower.

Buttercup (cut in half)

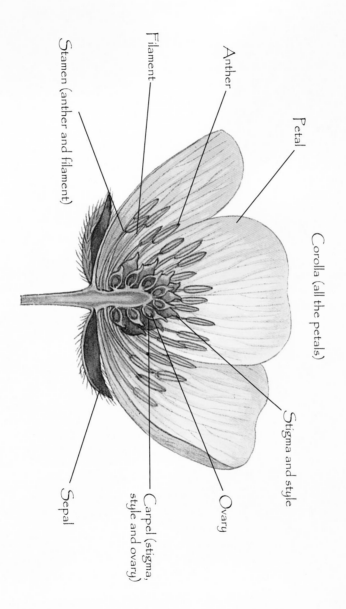

Petal

Corolla (all the petals)

Anther

Stigma and style

Filament

Ovary

Stamen (anther and filament)

Carpel (stigma, style and ovary)

Sepal

Garden flowers ~ blue

Periwinkle

Periwinkle

Length: 1m (3¼ft)
Spring to summer

This is a creeping plant – the trailing stems put down roots where they touch the soil, and then grow flowering shoots. Periwinkles like shade.

WHEN ....
WHERE ....

Morning glory

Height: up to 3m (10ft)
Summer

Morning glory is a climbing plant which has heart-shaped leaves. Its large, trumpet-shaped flowers last only a day. They look best in the morning and close up later in the day.

WHEN ....
WHERE ....

Morning glory

Grape hyacinth

Height: 10–18cm (4–7in)
Spring

Grape hyacinth is a small plant often used in flowerbeds. Its tiny flowers form a spike and it has strap-like leaves and bell-shaped flowers. It grows from a bulb.

WHEN ....
WHERE ....

Grape hyacinth

Delphinium

Height: 45–65cm (17¾–25½in)
Summer

Delphiniums are herbaceous plants. This means they have soft, not woody, stems. They have deeply-toothed leaves and a long spike of flowers with small flowering side shoots. Their flowers can also be mauve or white.

WHEN ....
WHERE ....

Delphinium

Love-in-a-mist

Height: 40cm (15¾in)
Summer

This plant has delicate, fern-like leaves on its stems and around its flowers. The flowers can also be pink or white.

WHEN ....
WHERE ....

Love-in-a-mist

Hibiscus

Height: 2–3m (6½–10ft)
Summer to autumn

Hibiscus grows as a bush with large, single flowers which don't last very long. Its leaves have three lobes with rounded teeth. It is a deciduous plant – it loses its leaves in winter.

WHEN ....
WHERE ....

Lobelia

Lobelia

Height: 9–22cm (3½–8¾in)
Summer

Lobelia is a small plant often used in flowerbeds, as it spreads easily. It has narrow, toothed leaves, with many small, delicate flowers.

WHEN ....
WHERE ....

Bell flower

Height: 8–20cm (3–8in)
Summer

There are several varieties of bell flower. As their name suggests, their flowers are shaped like bells.

WHEN ....
WHERE ....

Forget-me-not

Height: 23cm (9in)
Spring

This plant is often used as ground cover – to spread over the earth below taller plants. Its leaves are coated with fine hairs. The small flowers can also be white or pink.

WHEN ....
WHERE ....

African lily

Height: 60–90cm (23½–35½in)
Summer

This plant has around 35 flowers in a rounded head. It has many long, wide, thick leaves at the base, but none on the stems. It is often used as a pot plant and likes a sunny position.

WHEN ....
WHERE ....

Garden flowers ~ purple

Pasque flower

Height: 10cm (4in)
Spring

This plant, which is rare in the wild, has hairy, feathery leaves. The flowers can also be white.

WHEN ....
WHERE ....

Pasque flower

Lilac

Height: 2.5–3.5m (8–11½ft)
Late spring

Lilac can grow as a large, upright bush or as a small tree. It has bunches of tiny, scented flowers. Each flower has four petals and the leaves are heart-shaped.

WHEN ....
WHERE ....

Lilac

Wisteria

Height: up to 10m (33ft)
Spring to summer

Scented bunches of flowers hang from this climbing bush. The leaves are oval and pointed. Wisteria is often seen growing up walls.

WHEN ....
WHERE ....

Wisteria

Purple aubrieta

Height: 7–10cm (2¾–4in)
Spring

Look for this plant on walls or in rock gardens. The flowers are small and have four rounded petals. The leaves are toothed and hairy.

WHEN ....
WHERE ....

Purple
aubrieta

Rosemary

Height: up to 1.5m (5ft)
Summer

Rosemary is used as a herb in cooking. Its small flowers have a lip that insects use to land on. Its leaves are needle-like.

Rosemary

WHEN ....
WHERE ....

Garden flowers ~ pink

Rhododendron

Height: 3–4.5m (10–15ft)
Spring to summer

Rhododendron bushes are evergreen. This means they keep their leaves in winter. The flower heads are made up of funnel-shaped flowers, which are around 7cm (2¼in) across and come in different colours.

WHEN ....
WHERE ....

Rhododendron

Pink magnolia

Pink magnolia

Height: 3–5m (10–16ft)
Spring

This is a large, woody bush that has goblet-shaped flowers, with petals that drop off easily. The flowers bloom on bare branches and the leaves appear later.

WHEN ....
WHERE ....

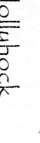

Hollyhock

Hollyhock

Height: 1.5m (5ft)
Summer

Hollyhocks are tall with a spike of flowers. The flowers may be colours other than pink. Their leaves are rough and hairy. They like to grow in a sunny position.

WHEN ....
WHERE ....

Pink

Height: 12–30cm (4¾–12in)
Summer

Pinks have flat, fragrant flowers with fringed petals, which last a long time. The stems and leaves are greyish-white, and the leaves are narrow and pointed. The colour pink is named after the flower.

WHEN ....
WHERE ....

Pink

Camellia

Height: 2–2.5m (6½–8ft)
Late winter to mid-spring

The flowers of the camellia are cup-shaped and can also be red or white. Frost can easily damage them. Camellia bushes have dark, glossy leaves and are evergreen.

WHEN ....
WHERE ....

Camellia

Garden flowers ~ red

Red hot poker

Height: 90cm (35½in)
Summer

Red hot pokers have long, narrow, pointed leaves. Their tube-shaped, downward-pointing flowers grow close together on poker-like spikes.

WHEN ....
WHERE ....

Red hot poker

Fuchsia

Length: up to 1m (3¼ft)
Summer to autumn

Fuchsia ("few-shuh") plants have drooping flowers. Their inner petals form a bell and are usually a different colour from the outer petals. They are bushy, and often grown in pots.

WHEN ....
WHERE ....

Fuchsia

Oriental poppy

Height: 70cm (27½in)
Early summer

Look for the black marks at the base of the large, waxy petals of this plant. It has hairy stems and leaves, and the stigmas and stamens are easy to see.

WHEN ....
WHERE ....

Oriental poppy

Geranium

Height: 50cm (19¾in)
Summer

Geraniums are often used as pot plants. They have rounded, pale green leaves with darker rings. The large head of flowers can be many different colours.

WHEN ....
WHERE ....

Geranium

Moyes' rose

Height: up to 2m (6½ft)
Mid-summer

This is a tall rose bush. The flowers are followed by shiny, red fruit that look like small bottles. The stem is usually thinner than that of the hybrid tea rose (see page 65).

WHEN ....
WHERE ....

Moyes' rose

Garden flowers ~ orange

Montbretia

Height: 60cm (23½in)
Late summer

The delicate flowers of this plant grow in long spikes. It has long, narrow, pointed leaves, which have raised ribs. The leaves grow from the base. It spreads easily.

WHEN ....
WHERE ....

Montbretia

Globe flower

Height: 60cm (23½in)
Summer

These globe-shaped flowers are like huge buttercups. The leaves have toothed lobes. It is often used in borders or at the sides of ponds.

WHEN ....
WHERE ....

Globe flower

Azalea

Height: 0.5–3m (1½–10ft)
Spring to summer

This evergreen bush has clusters of bell-shaped flowers and oval, pointed leaves. The flowers have long styles and stamens and usually have a strong scent.

WHEN ....
WHERE ....

Azalea

Nasturtium

Height: 20–40cm (8–15¾in)
Summer to autumn

This is a climbing and trailing plant, with scented, trumpet-shaped flowers. The leaves have wavy edges and smell like cabbages.

WHEN ....
WHERE ....

Nasturtium

Pot marigold

Height: 30–40cm (12–15¾in)
Summer to autumn

This bushy plant is an "annual", which means it lives for a year. It has large, daisy-like flowers and hairy, oval leaves. It is grown in borders and in pots. The petals may close at night.

WHEN ....
WHERE ....

Pot marigold

Garden flowers ~ white

Japanese anemone

Height: 75–90cm (29½–35½in)
Late summer

Japanese anemone flowers grow in groups on long, branching stems. The leaves at the base of the stem are deeply lobed.

WHEN ....
WHERE ....

Japanese anemone

Rock cress

Height: 20cm (8in)
Spring to summer

This is a small, evergreen plant which grows on walls and banks. It has long, rounded leaves. Each small flower has four petals and is sweetly scented.

WHEN ....
WHERE ....

Rock cress

Laurustinus

Height: 2–3m (6½–10ft)
Winter to spring

This is an evergreen bush with pointed, oval leaves. The small flowers make a flat head. It has a sweet smell.

WHEN ....
WHERE ....

Laurustinus

Snowdrop

Snowdrop

Height: 7–18cm (2¾–7in)
Winter to spring

This plant has drooping flowers with three, short inner petals and three, long outer ones. It has long, flat, strap-shaped leaves.

WHEN ....
WHERE ....

Mock orange

Mock orange

Height: 2–2.5m (6½–8ft)
Summer

This is a large, woody bush with small cup-shaped flowers. It smells sweet and its petals drop easily.

WHEN ....
WHERE ....

Christmas rose

Height: 30–45cm (12–17¾in)
Winter

This plant has saucer-shaped flowers and tough, dark, evergreen leaves. It likes to be partly shaded, where it is protected from winter frosts.

WHEN ....
WHERE ....

Christmas rose

Chrysanthemum

Height: 60–90cm (23½–35½in)
Summer

This is a herbaceous plant, which means it has a soft stem, rather than a woody one. It has large, daisy-like flowers with yellow middles. Its leaves are smooth and toothed.

WHEN ....
WHERE ....

Chrysanthemum

Wedding bells

Height: 2–3m (6½–10ft)
Mid-summer

This bushy plant has branches growing straight up with peeling bark. Its flowers grow in clusters.

WHEN ....
WHERE ....

Wedding bells

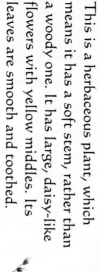

Lily of the valley

Height: 15–18cm (6–7in)
Spring

Lily of the valley has arching stems, each with five to twenty sweet-smelling, bell-shaped, waxy flowers. It also has pairs of broad leaves, and red fruit.

WHEN ....
WHERE ....

Lily of the valley

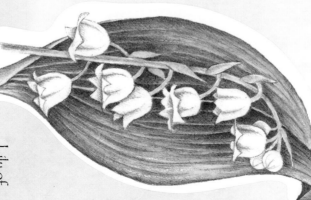

Baby's breath

Height: 90cm (35½in)
Summer

Also known as gypsophila, this plant has many star-shaped flowers and narrow, pointed leaves. It is bushy and dome-shaped.

WHEN ....
WHERE ....

Baby's breath

Garden flowers ~ yellow

Cone flower

Cone flower

Height: 1m (3¼ft)
Late summer

This plant gets its name from the raised green cones which rise up from the middle of the flowers. The petals point down.

WHEN ....

WHERE ....

Daffodil

Height: 15–60cm (6–23½in)
Spring

Daffodils usually have one flower on each stem. It has six, flat petals and a trumpet-shaped cup. The leaves are strap-shaped.

WHEN ....

WHERE ....

Daffodil

Broom

Height: 2.5m (8ft)
Early summer

This sweet-scented, upright bush has green stems and tiny leaves. It has many flowers, which grow on their own or in pairs.

WHEN ....

WHERE ....

Broom

Golden rod

Height: up to 2m (6½ft)
Summer to autumn

The tiny, feathery flowers of golden rod grow in clusters. The plant has long leaves that are rough on top, and grow at alternate points up the stem. It is often grown in sunny borders.

WHEN ....

WHERE ....

Golden rod

Sunflower

Height: 1.5–3m (5–10ft)
Summer

This plant has heart-shaped leaves and hairy stems. The single flowers are up to 35cm (13¼in) across.

WHEN ....

WHERE ....

Sunflower

Wallflower

Height: 30–60cm (12–23½in)
Late spring

This is an upright, bushy plant. The sweet-smelling flowers can be other colours. It has long, smooth leaves and likes to grow in sunny borders.

WHEN ....

WHERE ....

Evening primrose

Evening primrose

Height: 1.5m (5ft)
Summer

The scented, funnel-shaped flowers of this plant open in the evening. The leaves are long, deeply-veined, and have marks underneath.

WHEN ....

WHERE ....

Wallflower

Winter jasmine

Height: up to 3m (10ft)
Summer

Winter jasmine flowers are small and trumpet-shaped. They appear before the leaves. The plant has a tough, dark-green stem and small, glossy leaves. It can be trained to grow up walls.

WHEN ....

WHERE ....

Honeysuckle

Height: 2–3m (6½–10ft)
Summer

This plant has long, scented, tube-shaped flowers which grow in clusters. It bears poisonous fruit in the autumn.

WHEN ....

WHERE ....

Honeysuckle

Winter jasmine

Forsythia

Height: 2.5m (8ft)
Early spring

This plant has star-shaped flowers in clusters. Long, toothed leaves appear after the flowers.

WHEN ....

WHERE ....

Forsythia

Garden flowers ~ mixed

Clematis

Sweet pea

Hyacinth

Height: 30–50cm (12–19¾in)
Early spring

Hyacinths have many small, waxy, sweet-smelling flowers on one or two thick stems. Long, narrow leaves grow from the bulb of the plants. They are often grown in pots and window boxes.

WHEN ....
WHERE ....

Hyacinth

Clematis

Height: 1.5–3m (5–10ft)
Summer

This is a climbing plant, which is used to cover walls and fences. The flowers can be purple, blue, yellow, orange, pink or white. It has oval leaves.

WHEN ....
WHERE ....

Petunia

Height: 30–45cm (12–17¾in)
Summer

Petunias are often grown in hanging baskets and also in window boxes. They have large, open, trumpet-shaped flowers. The leaves are oval and pointed.

WHEN ....
WHERE ....

Petunia

Snapdragon

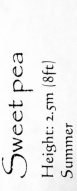

Sweet pea

Height: 2.5m (8ft)
Summer

The flowers are highly scented and can be many different colours. The leaves grow in pairs and the plant has tendrils that help it to climb.

WHEN ....
WHERE ....

Snapdragon

Height: 60cm (23½in)
Spring to autumn

The tube-shaped flowers of snapdragons grow in spikes. Look for this plant in garden borders.

WHEN ....
WHERE ....

Hybrid
tea rose

Hybrid tea rose

Height: up to 1.5m (5ft)
All summer

This rose has sweet-smelling flowers with cone-shaped buds. The stems have prickly thorns, and the leaves are glossy and grow in groups of three or five. Orange fruits, called rose hips, grow in the autumn.

WHEN ....

WHERE ....

Pansy

Height: 15–22cm (6–8¾in)
All year

Pansy flowers have five petals. They can be many different colours and usually have dark middles. This plant is commonly grown in hanging baskets. Some pansies flower in the winter.

WHEN ....

WHERE ....

Pansy

Lupin

Height: up to 1.5m (5ft)
Summer

This plant has a spike of small flowers. Its leaves are made up of five to fifteen leaflets. It is often grown in borders.

WHEN ....

WHERE ....

Dahlia

Dahlia

Height: 30–90cm (12–35½in)
Late summer

Dahlia ("daily-uh") flowers are globe-shaped, formed by rings of petals with a dark middle. They are used in borders, and there are many types.

WHEN ....

WHERE ....

Lupin

Foxglove

Height: up to 1.5m (5ft)
Summer

Foxgloves are tall with a long spike. Their spotted, bell-shaped flowers usually grow on only one side of the spike. Large, rough leaves grow from the base.

WHEN ....

WHERE ....

Foxglove

Wild flowers ~ white

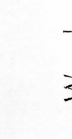

Wood anemone

Clover

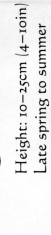

Shepherd's purse

Shepherd's purse

Height: up to 40cm (15¾in)
All year

Shepherd's purse is a very common plant. Its white flowers and heart-shaped seed pods can be seen all year.

WHEN ....
WHERE ....

Wood anemone

Height: 15cm (6in)
Spring to summer

This plant is also called Grammy's nightcap. It grows in large patches in woods. The flowers have pink-streaked sepals.

WHEN ....
WHERE ....

White dead-nettle

White dead-nettle

Height: up to 60cm (23½in)
Early summer to winter

This plant looks like an ordinary nettle, but its leaves do not sting. The flowers grow in whorls on the stem. It is found in hedgerows and on waste ground.

WHEN ....
WHERE ....

Daisy

Daisy

Height: 10cm (4in)
All year, except mid-winter

Daisies are small plants with a rosette of leaves at the base. Their name comes from "day's eye", as the flowers close at night (and in bad weather). They are very common on garden lawns.

WHEN ....
WHERE ....

Clover

Height: 10–25cm (4–10in)
Late spring to summer

The leaves of this creeping plant have three leaflets (sections). The flowers attract bees.

WHEN ....
WHERE ....

White campion

Height: up to 1m (3¼ft)
Late spring to summer

The stems and sepals of the white campion are sticky and hairy. The petals are divided. This plant grows in hedgerows.

WHEN ....

WHERE ....

Wild garlic

Height: 10–25cm (4–10in)
Late spring to summer

This plant smells strongly of garlic. Its broad, bright green leaves grow from a bulb. It grows in large patches in damp woods, often with bluebells (see page 70).

WHEN ....

WHERE ....

Wild garlic

Scented mayweed

Height: 15–40cm (6–15¾in)
All summer

This plant is found on waste ground everywhere. It has finely divided leaves and its petals fold back.

WHEN ....

WHERE ....

Scented mayweed

Cow parsley

Height: up to 1m (3¼ft)
All summer

This plant is also called Lady's lace. Look for the ribbed stem, feathery leaves and white flower clusters. It is found on banks and in ditches.

WHEN ....

WHERE ....

Cow parsley

Greater stitchwort

Height: 15–60cm (6–23½in)
Spring to summer

Look in woods and hedgerows for this slender, creeping plant. It has grass-like leaves and split petals.

WHEN ....

WHERE ....

Greater stitchwort

Wild flowers ~ yellow

Creeping Jenny

Height: 1m (3¼ft)
Summer

This creeping plant grows in a mat over the ground. It has shiny, oval leaves. It grows in damp, grassy places and under hedges.

WHEN ....
WHERE ....

Creeping Jenny

Rape

Height: up to 1m (3¼ft)
Summer

This plant is common on waysides and in fields. It is grown for the vegetable oil that is made from its seeds, and as winter feed for cattle. Look for its long seed pods.

WHEN ....
WHERE ....

Rape

Cowslip

Height: 15cm (6in)
Early summer

Cowslips have single clusters of nodding flowers, with a rosette of leaves at the base. They grow in meadows.

WHEN ....
WHERE ....

Cowslip

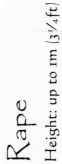

Gorse

Gorse

Height: 1–2m (3¼–6¼ft)
Spring to summer

Gorse is also called furze or whin. It is a dark-green, spiny bush, which is found on heaths and commons. The flowers smell like almonds.

WHEN ....
WHERE ....

Primrose

Height: 15cm (6in)
Winter to late spring

"Primrose" means "first rose" as this is often the first flower of spring. It has hairy stems and a rosette of large leaves. It often grows in patches in woods, hedges and fields.

WHEN ....
WHERE ....

Primrose

Lesser celandine

Height: 7cm (2¾in)
Spring to early summer

Lesser celandine has glossy, heart-shaped leaves and shiny flowers. It is a small, creeping plant that is often found in shady woods and waysides.

WHEN ....

WHERE ....

Lesser
celandine

Creeping buttercup

Height: 0.5m (1½ft)
Summer

Look for the long, trailing stems of this plant, near to the ground. It has shiny flowers and is common in grassy places. Its leaves are hairy and deeply divided.

WHEN ....

WHERE ....

Creeping
buttercup

Bird's foot trefoil

Height: 10cm (4in)
Summer

The flowers of this small, creeping plant are streaked with red. Look for it on grassy banks and downs.

WHEN ....

WHERE ....

Bird's foot
trefoil

Dandelion

Height: 15cm (6in)
Spring to summer

Dandelions are very common. They have a rosette of toothed leaves and their flowers close at night. Look for the "clock" of downy white parachutes which carry the seeds.

WHEN ....

WHERE ....

Dandelion

Yellow
archangel

Yellow archangel

Height: 40cm (15¾in)
Summer

Yellow archangel ("ark-angel") has red-brown markings on its yellow petals. It has opposite pairs of leaves and is common in woods.

WHEN ....

WHERE ....

Wild flowers ~ blue

Meadow sage

Meadow sage

Height: 40cm (15¾in)
Summer

Also called meadow clary, it has a hairy stem with wrinkled leaves mainly at the base. It grows in grassy places. Very rare.

WHEN ....
WHERE ....

Chicory

Height: 60cm (23½in)
Summer

This plant grows in grassy places and on waste ground. Its stems are branched and tufted, and the flowers grow in clusters.

WHEN ....
WHERE ....

Chicory

Speedwell

Speedwell

Height: 30cm (12in)
Summer

This is a hairy plant which grows in large mats over the ground. Pinkish-blue flowers grow on upright spikes. The leaves grow opposite each other. It is found in grassy places and woods.

WHEN ....
WHERE ....

Sea holly

Sea holly

Height: 50cm (19¾in)
Summer

Sea holly is a stiff, spiny plant with grey-blue leaves and round flower heads. Look for it on sandy and shingle beaches.

WHEN ....
WHERE ....

Bluebell

Bluebell

Height: 30cm (12in)
Spring to early summer

Bluebells are also called wild hyacinths. They have narrow, shiny leaves and clusters of nodding, deep violet-blue flowers. They grows in thick carpets in woods. Spanish bluebells are also seen, even in Britain: they are pale blue, pink or white, and have broader leaves.

WHEN ....
WHERE ....

Larkspur

Height: 50cm (19¾in)
Summer

This slender plant has divided, feathery leaves. The flowers have a long spur at the back. It grows mainly on wasteland.

WHEN ....
WHERE ....

Harebell

Viper's bugloss

Height: 30cm (12in)
Summer to autumn

This plant has long, narrow leaves on rough, hairy stems. It can either grow straight up or as a creeping plant. Pink buds become blue flowers. It is found on waysides and sand dunes.

WHEN ....
WHERE ....

Viper's bugloss

Larkspur

Blue flax

Height: 30cm (12in)
Spring to summer

This plant is found on dry grassland, in areas where the earth is made up of chalk or limestone. The leaves are slender.

WHEN ....
WHERE ....

Harebell

Height: 10–25cm (4–10in)
Late spring to summer

Harebells are found on dry grassland and heaths. The leaves are at the bottom of the plant are round and flat. Those at the top are slender and narrow. In Scotland, they are often called bluebells.

WHEN ....
WHERE ....

Cornflower

Cornflower

Height: 40cm (15¾in)
Summer

This plant has greyish, downy leaves. It grows in cornfields and on waste ground. It is fairly rare, and also called the bluebottle.

WHEN ....
WHERE ....

Blue flax

Wild flowers ~ purple and red

Scarlet
pimpernel

Common teasel

Height: 70cm (27½in)
Summer

Common teasels are often found on waste ground. In winter, they are brown and brittle. The head is made up of lots of tiny flowers. Those around the middle of the head flower first.

WHEN ....

WHERE ....

Common
teasel

Snake's head fritillary

Height: 10cm (4in)
Early summer

The drooping flowers of this rare plant are usually chequered with light and dark purple, but its colour can vary from purple to white. It grows in damp meadows.

WHEN ....

WHERE ....

Scarlet pimpernel

Height: 15cm (6in)
Summer

Scarlet pimpernel flowers open in the morning and close by mid-afternoon, or in bad weather. It has black dots under its pointed, oval leaves, and grows on farmland.

WHEN ....

WHERE ....

Snake's head
fritillary

Field scabious

Height: 15–30cm (6–12in)
Summer to autumn

This plant has narrow, pointed leaves. The flowers are pale to dark purple, with round heads. It grows in dry, grassy places.

WHEN ....

WHERE ....

Field
scabious

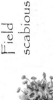

Common dog violet

Height: 10cm (4in)
Spring to summer

This is a creeping plant with rosettes of heart-shaped leaves. Look for its pointed sepals. It is commonly found in woods.

WHEN ....

WHERE ....

Common
dog violet

Tufted vetch

Height: 0.5–2m (1½–6½ft)
Summer to autumn

This is a scrambling plant which has clinging tendrils. It climbs up hedgerows. Look for the brown seed pods in late summer.

WHEN ....

WHERE ....

Tufted
vetch

Ivy-leaved toadflax

Height: 0.5m (1½ft)
Summer to autumn

The weak, slender stalks of the ivy-leaved toadflax trail on old walls. Look for the yellow lips on the flowers. The leaves are shiny.

WHEN ....

WHERE ....

Ivy-leaved toadflax

Common poppy

Height: up to 60cm (23½in)
Summer

Common poppies have stiff hairs on their stems. Their soft flowers have dark middles and their seed pods are round. They are found in cornfields and on waste ground.

WHEN ....

WHERE ....

Common
poppy

Sea lavender

Height: 30cm (12in)
Summer

This plant is found in saltmarshes, which are areas made of sand and salty mud. The leaves have long stalks. The flowers grow in clusters of between seven and ten.

WHEN ....

WHERE ....

Sea
lavender

Nettle-leaved bellflower

Height: 30cm (12in)
Summer to autumn

Also called bats-in-the-belfry, this is a hairy plant with large, toothed leaves. Its flowers point up on leafy spikes. It grows in hedges, woods and shady places.

WHEN ....

WHERE ....

Nettle-leaved
bellflower

Wild flowers ~ pink

Bell heather

Height: 30cm (12in)
Summer

Bell heather has thin, needle-shaped leaves and clusters of bell-shaped flowers. It grows on dry heaths and moors.

WHEN ....
WHERE ....

Bell heather

Ragged robin

Height: 30–70cm (12–27½in)
Early summer

This plant has a forked stem and narrow, pointed leaves. Its flowers have ragged, pink petals. It can be seen in damp meadows, marshes and woods.

WHEN ....
WHERE ....

Ragged robin

Early purple orchid

Height: up to 60cm (23½in)
Summer

This plant has dark spots on its leaves. It smells like cats, and is found in wooded areas.

WHEN ....
WHERE ....

Early purple orchid

Greater bindweed

Height: 3m (10ft)
Summer to autumn

Look for the large, pale pink or white, funnel-shaped flowers of this plant. It climbs walls and hedges on waste ground. The leaves are shaped like arrowheads.

WHEN ....
WHERE ....

Greater bindweed

Soapwort

Height: 40cm (15¾in)
Late summer to autumn

This plant has clusters of scented flowers (often with double flowers). The broad, oval leaves were once used to make soap. It grows near rivers and streams.

WHEN ....
WHERE ....

Soapwort

Blackberry

Blackberry

Height: 1m (3¼ft)
Summer to autumn

Blackberry (also called bramble) is a dense, woody plant that climbs up hedges. It has sharp prickles on the stems and under its leaves. The berries are ripe in autumn.

WHEN ....
WHERE ....

Dog rose

Height: up to 3m (10ft)
Mid-summer

This is a shrubby plant with thorny stems. It grows in hedges and woods. Look for its fruit of red rose hips in the autumn.

WHEN ....
WHERE ....

Dog rose

Bloody cranesbill

Height: 30cm (12in)
Mid-summer

Also called bloody-red geranium, this plant is bushy, with trailing stems. Its deeply-divided leaves are round and hairy. It grows in hedgerows and grasslands, and on cliffs.

WHEN ....
WHERE ....

Herb
Robert

Herb Robert

Height: 40cm (15¾in)
Early to late summer

This is a spreading plant, which has a strong smell. The flowers droop at night and in bad weather. The leaves become red in the autumn. It lives in woods and on the banks of hedgerows.

WHEN ....
WHERE ....

Bloody
cranesbill

Red campion

Height: 60cm (23½in)
Early summer

Red campion has a hairy, sticky stem. The pointed, oval leaves grow in opposite pairs.

WHEN ....
WHERE ....

Red campion

Flowers checklist

This list will help you find every flower in the book. The first number after each flower tells you which page it is on. The second number (in brackets) is the number of the sticker.

African lily 55 (61)
Azalea 59 (103)
Baby's breath 61 (46)
Bats-in-the-belfry (see Nettle-leaved bellflower)
Bell flower 55 (10)
Bell heather 74 (92)
Bird's foot trefoil 69 (67)
Blackberry 75 (58)
Bloody cranesbill 75 (40)
Bluebell 70 (32)
Blue flax 71 (97)
Broom 62 (49)
Camellia 57 (47)
Chicory 70 (11)
Christmas rose 61 (109)
Chrysanthemum 61 (22)
Clematis 64 (4)
Clover 66 (53)
Common dog violet 72 (3)
Common poppy 73 (107)
Common teasel 72 (48)
Cone flower 62 (94)
Cornflower 71 (21)
Cow parsley 67 (45)
Cowslip 68 (9)
Creeping buttercup 69 (88)
Creeping Jenny 68 (6)

Daffodil 62 (76)
Dahlia 65 (63)
Daisy 66 (56)
Dandelion 69 (82)
Delphinium 54 (28)
Dog rose 75 (65)
Early purple orchid 74 (19)
Evening primrose 63 (44)
Field scabious 72 (95)
Forget-me-not 55 (15)
Forsythia 63 (7)
Foxglove 65 (87)
Fuchsia 58 (20)
Geranium 58 (34)
Globe flower 59 (85)
Golden rod 62 (51)
Gorse 68 (93)
Grape hyacinth 54 (33)
Greater bindweed 74 (84)
Greater stitchwort 67 (24)
Harebell 71 (71)
Herb Robert 75 (77)
Hibiscus 55 (59)
Hollyhock 57 (1)
Honeysuckle 63 (86)
Hyacinth 64 (12)
Hybrid tea rose 65 (62)
Ivy-leaved toadflax 73 (89)

Japanese anemone 60 (2)
Larkspur 71 (81)
Laurustinus 60 (78)
Lesser celandine 69 (17)
Lilac 56 (36)
Lily of the valley 61 (110)
Lobelia 55 (104)
Love-in-a-mist 54 (79)
Lupin 65 (75)
Meadow sage 70 (66)
Mock orange 60 (72)
Montbretia 59 (69)
Morning glory 54 (91)
Moyes' rose 58 (8)
Nasturtium 59 (64)
Nettle-leaved bellflower 73 (23)
Oriental poppy 58 (5)
Pansy 65 (108)
Pasque flower 56 (68)
Periwinkle 54 (90)
Petunia 64 (73)
Pink 57 (38)
Pink magnolia 57 (13)
Pot marigold 59 (98)
Primrose 68 (57)
Purple aubrieta 56 (80)
Ragged robin 74 (30)
Rape 68 (31)

Red campion 75 (18)
Red hot poker 58 (25)
Rhododendron 57 (60)
Rock cress 60 (52)
Rosemary 56 (55)
Scarlet pimpernel 72 (50)
Scented mayweed 67 (83)
Sea holly 70 (54)
Sea lavender 73 (39)
Shepherd's purse 66 (70)
Snake's head fritillary 72 (74)
Snapdragon 64 (35)
Snowdrop 60 (26)
Soapwort 74 (100)
Speedwell 70 (41)
Sunflower 74 (99)
Sweet pea 64 (96)
Tufted vetch 73 (37)
Viper's bugloss 71 (106)
Wallflower 63 (14)
Wedding bells 61 (29)
White campion 67 (102)
White dead-nettle 66 (42)
Wild garlic 67 (16)
Winter jasmine 63 (27)
Wisteria 56 (101)
Wood anemone 66 (105)
Yellow archangel 69 (43)

Plant words

Annual – a plant that lives only for one year

Anther – the end of a stamen that makes pollen (male cells)

Bedding plant – a low-growing annual plant, used in flowerbeds to cover the ground

Bulb – a short underground stem with fleshy leaves. It stores food for the leaves, and surrounds the flower bud of some plants, such as daffodils.

Carpel – the female reproductive parts of a plant

Deciduous – a tree or shrub that sheds all its leaves every year at the end of the growing season

Evergreen – a tree or shrub that is covered with leaves all year

Filament – the stalk of a stamen

Herbaceous – a plant with a fleshy, not woody, stem

Lobed – a type of leaf. Its divided parts have round edges.

Ovary – the enlarged part of a carpel, containing female cells

Rosette – a circular cluster of leaves, growing from the base of the stem

Sepals – leaf-like structures which protect the reproductive parts of a plant

Shrub – a woody plant, smaller than a tree, with several branches growing from near the base

Stigma – the sticky upper portion of the carpel

Style – the long portion of the carpel that joins the stigma to the ovary

Tendril – a thread-like leaf or stem that attaches climbing plants to a wall, fence or other plant, by twining around it, or sticking to it

Whorl – a circle of three or more petals or leaves around a stem

37

38

39

40

41

42

43

44

45

46

47

58

61

65

64

62

59

66

60

67

63

71

74

77

79

70

69

79

73

76

75

78

68

72

78

83

86

88

80

80

81

84

89

87

82

90

85

91

92

93

94

95

96

97

98

99

100

101

102

108

105

103

106

104

109

107

110